The Mystery of Joseph

THE MYSTERY OF JOSEPH

MARIE-DOMINIQUE PHILIPPE, O.P.

ZACCHEUS PRESS
Bethesda

THE MYSTERY OF JOSEPH. Originally published in French as *Le Mystère de Joseph* © Saint-Paul Editions Religieuses, 82 rue Bonaparte, 75006 Paris. Translation copyright © 2009 by the Community of St. John. Foreword, cover art and text, and endorsements copyright © 2010 by Zaccheus Press. All rights reserved. Printed in USA. No part of this book may be used or reproduced in any manner whatsoever without written permission except in the case of quotations in critical articles or reviews. For information address Zaccheus Press, 4605 Chase Avenue, Bethesda, Maryland 20814.

ZACCHEUS PRESS and the colophon are trademarks of Zaccheus Press. The Zaccheus Press colophon was designed by Michelle Dick.

Library of Congress Cataloging-in-Publication Data

Philippe, M.-D. (Marie-Dominique)
 [Mystère de Joseph. English]
 The mystery of Joseph / Marie-Dominique Philippe.
  p. cm.
 Includes bibliographical references (p.   ).
 ISBN 978-0-9725981-3-2 (pbk. : alk. paper)
 1. Joseph, Saint. I. Title.
 BS2458.P4813 2009
 232.9'32--dc22

                                                        2009041453

To learn more about Zaccheus Press, please visit our webpage:

www.zaccheuspress.com

Pater Misericordiae, emitte Spiritum Tuum ut omnium hunc librum legentium et mentum illuminet et cor tangat. Sit instrumentum ad exaedificandum Regnum Tuum. Per Christum Dominum nostrum. Amen.

CONTENTS

PART TWO
Living with Saint Joseph

APPENDIX

FOREWORD

by

Father Benedict J. Groeschel, C.F.R.

The publication of this serious, even profound study of a person intimately joined to the life of the Messiah and written by one of the most respected figures in our contemporary Catholic scene should cause serious attention to be paid to the often neglected figure of Saint Joseph.

Father Marie-Dominique Philippe, O.P., an important French theologian who died only in 2006, was a man whose thought was of great influence and depth. He was also a man greatly devoted to the Church who founded the Community of Saint John. This new community is now recognized in several countries as a very successful attempt to restore a vibrant spirituality to the religious life, which in many places has seemed moribund for years. The Brothers and Sisters of Saint John are a cause of hope to those who look ahead to the restoration of the authentic and powerful traditions of the religious life that have gotten lost in recent times. The Franciscan Friars and Sisters of the Renewal have welcomed them with joy.

Father Philippe's book on Saint Joseph is very consistent with the new biblical theology called for by Pope Benedict XVI. The author very impressively examines the sparse facts that we have concerning the life of Saint Joseph, teasing from them material that connects easily and well with a very impressive structure of theological teaching. This then becomes a means of providing a firm foundation for devotion to the Foster Father and Guardian of the Son of God.

Except for Christ and Saint Paul, New Testament figures attract little attention from the secular world and especially the secular media—even when they are in a kindly mood. Occasionally a small amount of attention is shown to the figure of the Blessed Mother but rarely is Saint Joseph or any of the Apostles mentioned. Even in cities named Saint Joseph or San José are the inhabitants really conscious of the fact that their hometown is actually named for a person—a person who played a role of immense importance in God's plan of redemption for humankind. This apparent obscurity finds at its root a kind of Protestantism that is focused intensely on the figure Christ and on the writings of Saint Paul, but which seems barely acquainted with Saint Joseph and even the Mother of God, herself. Catholic theology, which takes a less constricted view of such things, opened up a world of devotion to Saint Joseph the humble carpenter of Nazareth as well as to the Mother of God. How could it be otherwise? These are the figures who stood at the manger on the first Christmas; they are the ones to whom the care of the Word Incarnate was entrusted by God.

In recent years there has been a gradual but very welcome return to biblical theology and a simultaneous turning away from the overly exclusive use of the historical-critical method. In the wake of such changes there has also come a resurgence of interest in the figure of Saint Joseph. When we place the few facts that we have of him in the context of his personal responsibilities for the Messiah, we begin to move away from the shadowy figure presented in Scripture and discover a multi-dimensional person—one still wrapped in mystery, but one of great importance. Young

Catholics seeking more solid theological food than what is generally being fed to them through the historical-critical school alone will find in Father Philippe's book much to feed their spiritual lives and inspire their devotion.

Father Philippe has profoundly moved many of these intelligent and well educated young men and women, and quite a few of them have joined the community he founded.

The Community of Saint John now includes not only members from France but also from many parts of the world. The same spirit and insight that led Father Philippe to such success in the founding of this congregation can be found in his writings, which I recommend to all.

The Mystery of Joseph is a wonderful place to begin your appreciation of Father Philippe. His way of looking into Scripture and finding in it an inexhaustible theological reservoir is an inspiration to all. Read and enjoy and pray. Father Philippe will teach you much about Saint Joseph and much about your faith. When you're all finished you will be quite surprised to see how your vision of this great saint may have changed. Even if you've been devoted to Saint Joseph for many years, I feel safe in saying that in *The Mystery of Joseph* you will learn a great deal about Jesus' Foster Father's true and undying importance.

Editor's Note

The following pages are divided into two sections. Part One comprises a short piece written by Fr. Marie-Dominique Philippe which was originally the preface to a reissued edition of *Saint Joseph intime* by Charles Sauvé; Part Two contains a number of lectures on various important aspects of Saint Joseph's holiness.

The reader should note that the texts featured in Part Two were not written directly by the author himself, but have been transcribed from conferences or homilies given by him, and that we have tried to respect the flowing style of his spoken delivery. Since this collection of writings was not planned by the author, the reader should not be surprised to find that certain themes appear more than once; we have tried to avoid repetitions, but there are doubtless some remaining.

We have added footnotes containing references to the Church Fathers and some supplementary explanations borrowed from other lectures given by the author, as well as cross-references to his previously published works. Lastly, we have included an appendix which contains a relevant extract from Pope Leo XIII's encyclical *Quamquam pluries* (defining the place of Saint Joseph in the Economy of Salvation), the traditional Litanies of Saint Joseph and several other prayers, among which the well-known prayers to the saint from the Oratory of Saint Joseph in Montreal, Quebec.

PART ONE

THE MYSTERY OF JOSEPH

THE MYSTERY OF JOSEPH

There is a need today, probably more than ever, to examine in a theological way the person of Saint Joseph, that "righteous man"[1] who brings the Old Covenant to its completion and who is used by God in such a remarkable way to bring about the New Covenant.

Saint Joseph occupies, without doubt, a unique place within the Divine Economy, and plays a role which, while being essential, remains at the same time quite hidden. The Church, in her devotion to Saint Joseph (most notably in the litanies that she addresses to him), invokes him as "Father of Patriarchs," thus acknowledging a link between the patriarchs and Saint Joseph. It is this very link which is revealed to us in Matthew's Gospel when we are presented with the "genealogy of Jesus Christ, the son of David, the son of Abraham."[2] This section of the Gospel begins with Abraham and concludes with "Joseph, the husband of Mary, of whom was born Jesus, Who is called the Christ."[3] In Luke's Gospel also, Joseph is linked back to "Adam, son of God." The covenant made with Joseph is so deep-rooted that it is not enough to link him back only as far as Abraham; he must be linked all the way back to Adam himself.[4]

Joseph and Adam

Joseph is thus the one who connects Jesus with Abraham within the Divine Economy, and, in an even more radical way, he is the one who links Jesus back to Adam himself, across the entire span of human history.

This is what we need to discover. If we are to examine Joseph in a truly theological way, if we are to see this "righteous" man *as* God sees him, then we must discover this unique link, willed by God, between Joseph and the patriarchs, and even between Joseph and Adam. For just as Adam is the beginning of God's covenant with men (who are the little Benjamins of the great family of God, Creator and Father), and just as the patriarchs, by their faith in God's promise, are the beginning of a new covenant relationship, so too is Joseph, in faith, the beginning of the covenant *par excellence* between God and man, but in a way that is entirely different from the patriarchs—in a state of remarkable poverty, as we shall see. This covenant is a fulfillment of the covenant made with Abraham, and it is a radical renewal of all that has gone before, of all that has happened since Adam was driven out of Eden. Joseph is chosen by God to be the spouse of Mary, in whom the New Covenant will be brought about by the working of the Holy Spirit. He thereby becomes the father of Him Who is Himself the New Covenant, a covenant which is at once a fulfillment and a radical renewal of everything. Through Mary, Joseph is thus linked back to both Abraham and to Adam.

Joseph's Role in the New Covenant

When we are confronted with a great crisis, when we see "apocalyptic tremblings" (to use a phrase coined by Pope Paul VI), even within the Church, we need to return to the source. We must come back to the source, to the very beginning of the New Covenant, in order to differentiate more clearly, in the mystery of the Church (herself the fruit of this New Covenant) between what

God wills as absolutely necessary and that nothing can overpower, and those things which are the work of man—things which have been added secondarily over the centuries in the course of the Church's temporal pilgrimage.

And it is here at the source that we find the *mystery* of Joseph. For just as we cannot grasp anything of human history from the divine perspective without looking at Adam, nor anything of the mystery of Israel without looking at the faith of Abraham, in the same way we cannot grasp anything of the Church's development if we do not look at the mystery of Joseph. The Holy Spirit Himself has willed that this should be so, and He reveals it to us in the beginnings of the Gospels of Saint Matthew and Saint Luke.

In times of crisis—whether they be personal ones or those of a community—surely a return to the origin is needed, a return to what was chosen and desired at the beginning, in order to overcome the crisis with love and intelligence. This is perhaps the ultimate meaning of a crisis and the very reason that God allows it to happen. Thanks to this return to the source, we are able to obtain a clearer vision of the profound intentions and the profound finality of our personal vocation or of the vocation of a community. This return is not some sort of historical backtracking; it is not about reviving the past so as to relive it. It is a return to the source in order to discover what is essential in it, its *soul*: the inspiration, the true intention. Simple historical or sociological backtracking—i.e. a return in which we are nostalgic about the past and copy what was done—is always something that reduces things to a material level, for the only thing we can be nostalgic about and try to copy is the external behavior of a person or a community. Returning to the source to rediscover what is essential, on the other hand, is what gives rise to a new surge of life and love within us.

This is precisely why the Holy Spirit is asking the Church today to give special consideration to the mystery of Saint Joseph: to help the Church discover a light in this mystery that will allow her to move forward with a new surge of life and love.

Let us try, therefore, to sketch the essential features of a theology of Saint Joseph. In order to do so, let us return first of all to the passages in the Gospel that speak of him, and read them in the light of the Church's Tradition.

1. Joseph, Son of David, Spouse of Mary

Joseph's two claims to nobility are, firstly, that he is "of the house and line of David"[5] and, secondly, that Mary is betrothed to him. This is how he is first presented to us in the Gospels of Saint Matthew and Saint Luke. We know nothing of his life prior to this. We are told that his father's name was Jacob, who was himself the son of Matthan,[6] but we do not know anything about either Jacob or Matthan.

Joseph is of David's line. This is why, when the decree goes forth from Caesar Augustus that a census is to be made of "the whole world," Joseph has to go up from the town of Nazareth, in Galilee, "to the town of David, which is called Bethlehem," in Judea; and Mary, his betrothed, must go with him.[7] Here we see Joseph's roots in the People of Israel.

But who is David? The youngest son of Jesse of Bethlehem, David is chosen by the Lord because God does not judge as men judge, that is, seeing only what is obvious: "the Lord sees the heart."[8] Able to appease the wrath of Saul with his lyre,[9] David is also the one who volunteers to fight Goliath with his slingshot and who kills him.[10] Best friend of Jonathan, son of Saul,[11] David marries Michal, Saul's daughter, and is pursued by the latter with hatred and jealousy.[12] But David is also the king who, desiring Bathsheba, has no hesitation in sending her husband Uriah to his death so that he can marry her.[13] Nevertheless, despite this sin (for which he will atone greatly with the rebellion and death of his son Absalom), the Lord continues to bless David, giving him a second son, Solomon, by Bathsheba, after the death of his first son; of this son we are told that "the Lord loved him."[14] It is from this line that Joseph will be born. In Ecclesiasticus (Sirach), the greatness of David is proclaimed:

> As the fat is selected from the peace offering, so David was selected from the sons of Israel.... The Lord... gave him the covenant of kings and a throne of glory in Israel.[15]

Joseph is the son of David by royal descent, but he acquires a new and personal dignity when he becomes the husband of Mary. Scripture tells us nothing about how Joseph and Mary came to meet. How did Joseph discover her and come to love her? How did Mary come to accept his choice of her as his bride? How did she agree to be "betrothed" to him? Naturally, this providential encounter, willed by God, happened according to the customs of the day. The Holy Spirit did not disrupt these customs; He made use of them in a unique way so as to allow there to be a true and personal choice of reciprocal love between Joseph and Mary. They chose each other freely, loving each other and discovering, in this encounter, the providential action of God in each of their lives.

No other two persons have ever known an encounter so profound, of such simplicity and such intensity of love—a love which was, above all, divine, yet which did not destroy the human love which united them.[16] Saint Thomas has no hesitation in saying that there was a true marriage between Joseph and Mary because there existed between them "an inseparable union of souls."[17]

Mary's Consecration

If we look closely at Mary's question to the angel Gabriel when he announces to her that she will bear a son, the Son of the Most High—"How can this come about, since I know not man?"[18]—

we are led to discover, along with certain Church Fathers and medieval theologians, that Mary must have consecrated herself entirely to God before she met Joseph, but that this consecration had remained hidden. Mary could only have consecrated herself in such a way under the influence of the Holy Spirit, abandoning herself totally to the Father's gracious will, without seeking advice from anyone. We, moreover, who have received the Church's proclamation of the mystery of the Immaculate Conception, can (unlike the Church Fathers and the theologians for whom this mystery had not been proclaimed by the Church) recognize in Mary's consecration her first personal response to the freely given grace of the Immaculate Conception.

This response is carried out in the obscurity of her faith. In fact, Mary is unaware of the unique privilege that comes from God's love for her. Nonetheless, through the working of the Spirit, she responds by making a total gift of herself, so that God can embrace her all the more deeply with His prevenient mercy.

Joseph could not have known by himself that Mary had made a personal gift of herself to God in this way. But from the very moment Joseph chose Mary and loved her, Mary could only receive this choice and respond to it by communicating her secret to Joseph, telling him that she had surrendered herself totally to God's gracious will for her. Joseph must respect Mary's radical self-abandonment to the Father if he is to take her to be his wife. In choosing her as his wife, he must thus live the same mystery as she does—a mystery of self-abandonment and of total surrender of one's entire life into the hands of the Father. In becoming her spouse, he weds himself to the working of God's Spirit within her; he lives her secret, this secret which binds her so personally to the Father. Sharing the same intention is the foundation of their love of friendship[19]—a love which is so divine, so strong and so unique.

The whole of the Old Covenant, from Abraham to Joseph—

and, more fundamentally, the whole of God's covenant with Man—blossoms in this union, in this choice of predilection, in this mutual love. Neither Joseph nor Mary is aware of what this union represents within the Divine Economy, nor could they have been. They know, in the depths of their faith and in the consciences they have as believers (as "just" and God-fearing people),[20] that God is asking them to love each other. They are delighted to respond to this calling, which is both human and divine, and they surrender themselves totally to the gracious will of their God.

2. Joseph and the Divine Motherhood of Mary

The Annunciation

What is unique in the mystery of the Annunciation is that Mary, who is betrothed to Joseph, is nonetheless considered by God her Father to be totally free of commitments, as though she belonged to Him alone. Since she does, in fact, belong to Him alone, He is able do with her as He wills. The fact that she is betrothed to Joseph does not obstruct Mary's interior freedom to respond in love to God's gracious will.

Although God speaks only to Mary, even though she is betrothed to Joseph, He does not want to destroy the bond that unites them; He himself willed this bond. But He purifies it, makes it poor in spirit, gives it a new dimension.

Through the angel Gabriel, God addresses Mary directly and reveals to her how much He loves her—"*full* of grace"—how much His paternal favor rests upon her, and He asks her if she will accept to be the Mother of the "Son of the Most High." As for the "how," the *quomodo*—Mary does not see how this can happen since she has consecrated herself totally to God so as to be His alone—the angel asks Mary to surrender herself entirely to the Holy Spirit and to the power of the Most High: "The Holy

Spirit will come upon you, and the power of the Most High will overshadow you."[21] He gives her no word of explanation; He asks her to believe in the working of the Spirit within her, and to abandon herself totally to the power of the Most High, to live beneath His shadow.

In an act of love, and without taking advice from anyone, Mary declares her *fiat*: "Behold the handmaid of the Lord: be it done unto me according to Thy word."[22] Thus we see how the Father lovingly "steals" His little child: He wants her all for Himself and He asks her to cooperate in His work of love, in the gift of His beloved Son to mankind. Mary is the first to receive this gift, and she is to cooperate with it in a personal, maternal way. She is to receive this gift in total freedom and love; it is to give her greater freedom that the Father uses the angel Gabriel as His messenger. Mary receives this secret from the Father—the gift of His Son—in an act of faith, hope and love. She receives Him as a mother receives her son, in a mystery of divine fruitfulness. It is through this divine fruitfulness that the Father communicates the fruit of His eternal fecundity.

Mary is alone; she receives this gift in the solitude of her heart. She agrees to become a mother without asking Joseph's advice. She knows that God has every claim to her and that Joseph's deepest desire is that she belong entirely to her God.

It is not a lack of delicacy on her part to act in this way towards Joseph; rather it is a sign of her confidence in him. God must always come first, and this is the will of Joseph's heart as well—otherwise he would not be Mary's spouse. What is so admirable is that Mary does not hesitate, and in this she reveals to us all that Joseph's heart is for her: she can count on him even to this extent. She is able to keep God's secret in silence, for she does not doubt Joseph's faithfulness both to God and to herself.

One of the prefigurations of the Annunciation in the Old Testament is the annunciation made to the woman who would become Samson's mother, and it sheds a particular light on this aspect of Mary and Joseph's friendship. As soon as she receives the message from the "angel of God," the woman in the Old Testament prefiguration hurries to tell her husband, Manoah. Not entirely trusting her (and fearing that she has been seeing things), he considers it safer to ask the Lord for another annunciation: "O Lord, I pray Thee, let the man of God whom Thou didst send come again to us, and teach us what we are to do with the boy that will be born."[23] God grants this request and the angel reappears to the woman, who hurries to tell her husband. This prefiguration helps us to grasp better what is unique in the Annunciation to Mary. In Mary's Annunciation, the woman bears the burden of the promise alone. It is a secret of love; it is the gift of the beloved Son. Mary must receive it in a wholly loving faith and hope, and as she receives it she enters into the silence of the Word Who takes flesh within her. Through the silence of the tiny Child she carries within her, Mary enters into the silence of the Word.[24]

The angel gives her a sign: behold, Elizabeth who is barren and in her old age is with child, "for nothing is impossible for God." Mary, wise as she is, sees the meaning of this sign: she must go to Elizabeth "in haste" to assist her and to tell her of her love and her joy. This act of fraternal charity allows her to maintain more profoundly the silence desired by God.

Joseph's Trial

After passing three silent months with Elizabeth who, enlightened by the Spirit, understood everything, Mary returns to Joseph. The Gospel of Matthew reveals to us Joseph's disquiet:

> Before they came together she was found to be with child of the Holy Spirit; and her husband Joseph, being a just man and unwilling to put her to shame, resolved to send her away quietly. But

as he considered this, behold, an angel of the Lord appeared to him in a dream, saying, "Joseph, son of David, do not fear to take Mary your wife into your home, for that which is conceived in her is of the Holy Spirit; she will bear a son, and you shall call His name Jesus, for He will save His people from their sins." All this took place to fulfill what the Lord had spoken through the prophet: "Behold, a virgin shall conceive and bear a son, and his name shall be called Emmanuel," which means, God with us. When Joseph awoke from sleep, he did as the angel of the Lord commanded him; he took his wife into his home.[25]

Out of his love for Mary and his respect for the will of God, Joseph decides to give Mary back her liberty, and to do so with the utmost discretion. This is where we see Joseph's humility and poverty. He finds himself faced with the fact that God, without asking what he thinks about it, has been at work in Mary. He must therefore withdraw and leave Mary free so that God may continue to work in her and through her, as He wills.

The Evangelist emphasizes that, "All this took place to fulfill what the Lord had said through the prophet: 'Behold, the virgin shall conceive and bear a son.'" Is this not precisely in order to indicate that Joseph—who could doubt neither Mary's faithfulness nor loyalty towards him—had understood that the prophecy of Isaiah was being fulfilled in her?

Now this prophecy only spoke of a virgin conceiving and bearing a son; Joseph should therefore step aside. When Joseph had previously offered himself entirely to Mary, Mary had responded to this gift by explaining to him that God had every claim on her, and Joseph had accepted that. Now the time had come for him to respond in turn. He could not have known how quickly it would happen! Without looking back, Joseph makes his silent *fiat* to the will of His God. He accepts that Mary take precedence and that he withdraw into silence. The Virgin belongs to God alone and God has every claim on her. In Joseph's resolution we see the divine love that he has for Mary: he loves her *for herself*; he loves her in order that the will of God be fulfilled in her. He does not love her for himself; his love gives him no claim on her.

Joseph wants to do the will of God above all else. In his prudence, enlightened by faith and love, he makes this heroic decision out of love for Mary and out of respect for her.

But God has other plans, and the "angel of the Lord" explains this to him. This is Joseph's own annunciation. God does not have him participate in an explicit way in the Annunciation made to Mary, and this allowed God to test his heart: does he love the marvelous gift that God has given him—Mary—more than God's will for them both? Joseph had agreed to offer Mary to God; he had agreed to allow God to have an exclusive claim on the Virgin, to let Him take her far away from him, to take her even into the depths of His intimate relationship with His beloved Son, leaving Joseph himself far behind. So God sends His angel to Joseph to tell him of His trust in him and His love for him: "Joseph, son of David, do not fear to take Mary your wife into your home. For that which is conceived in her is of the Holy Spirit. She will bear a son, and you shall call His name Jesus."

Mary is told that she will conceive and bear the Son of the Most High, and Joseph is told that he must take Mary into his home—her who is carrying within her the One Who is to save His people and Who is the fruit of the Holy Spirit. The angel explains to Joseph that he is still to consider Mary in the same way: she is his wife. "For the gifts and the call of God are irrevocable."[26] He is not to distance himself from her. Indeed, she is given to him even more than before, for it is the Holy Spirit Who has been at work in her; he is therefore to consider Mary in a new light. He is to receive her in a more profound way, for he is to receive her in all her divine fruitfulness. He is also to receive the fruit of the Holy Spirit within her, for this fruit is given to him as well. The angel explains this to him by telling him that he himself is to give the Child the name "Jesus." Joseph is thus to exercise an authority over Mary (for she is his wife) and over the Child to Whom she will give birth: he is to give Him His name, as a father names his own son.

We can understand the joy in Joseph's heart, the joy in the heart of this man of poverty. He had surrendered everything to God and God rewards him a hundredfold. He had chosen Mary as his wife, and God gives him as his wife the mother of the Savior; and since everything belonging to Mary belongs to him, the fruit of her womb belongs to him also. Hence God gives him, through Mary, His own beloved Son to be *his* son also. For if Mary, his spouse, gives her son to him, it is so that He be *his* son also. Mary gives to Joseph all that the Father has given her. This is the Father's deepest desire for her, otherwise He would not have united Joseph to her as her spouse.

Joseph's Greatness and Poverty

Here we touch upon the magnanimity of Joseph in his poverty and humility. We can see now how he is a "son of David" and how he even surpasses his forefather in the royal authority conferred upon him by the Lord. Joseph accepted, in love, the real poverty which was demanded of him with regard to Mary's fruitfulness. He did not murmur within his heart; he did not lay claim to the legitimate right of husband over wife, for he had agreed right from the moment of their first meeting to have no human rights over Mary because she was God's alone, body and soul. He had agreed to have only such authority over her as the Father would give him. He truly marries her in the most complete poverty. This poverty, lived first of all in the intentions of his heart, is now lived effectively in the full realism of his human sensitivity. He accepts that God has brought about His master-piece within Mary, without including him, her spouse. He accepts that Mary alone will be the source of life for the formation of the body of the Son of the Most High become man, and he is even glad, because Mary is thus fully glorified and takes precedence over him: she is first.

As for Joseph himself, he agrees to cooperate in this unique work in the way that God wills. He accepts being poor with regard to the instinctive demands of flesh and blood in order to cooperate more fully, more lovingly and more divinely in his personal authority as a husband and father, and to do so with a love that is both human and divine, yet poor and without any rights. This is the wonderful way in which this man of poverty exercises his authority, and it enables him to be magnanimous—to behave like God Himself. It is truly his poverty and his magnanimity that allow him to exercise both his spousal authority over Mary, the masterpiece of Creation, and his paternal authority over He Who is the Son of God. The quality and the greatness of any authority are relative to the person over whom that authority is exercised; to have authority over the Son of God is a unique authority, similar to that of the "Father Who is in Heaven."

God the Father truly gives Joseph a unique authority, one which He had never given to anyone else, and He does so because He trusts Joseph and because He is "well-pleased" with him.[27] However He could only give him this authority once He had tested his heart. Indeed, it was in order to communicate to him this new love, this new authority, that He put him to the test.

Trusting in the Father, Joseph accepts this situation that is humanly impossible to live. Officially he is the spouse of Mary and the father of Jesus, and as a man and a believer he knows in his heart that he is the "faithful guardian" of the Virgin and of her Blessed Son, the Son of God. As the official spouse of Mary and father of Jesus, he hides the work of the Holy Spirit in Mary and the divine origin of his son Jesus from the eyes of all his people.[28] He must therefore accept to be the origin of the mistaken opinions that will be formed about Mary and Jesus.

This is perhaps the harshest trial for a just man. In order to live it with love and joy, he must fix his gaze solely on the will of the Father and not become fixed on his own human judgment or the judgments of others. He must live constantly in a radical conformity to the will of the Father, above and beyond all that comes from creatures.

This is where we touch upon the most profound aspect of Joseph's holiness: his love for Mary is so great that it now compels him to look at nothing else but the Father's will for her. His love for Jesus is so great that, like Jesus, he lives the accomplishment of the Father's will. In a state of total interior poverty, he must love Mary as the most tender, most gentle and attentive spouse, and with the greatest strength, whilst at the same time exercising an authority over her. He must love Jesus as a father, thinking only of Him and living only for Him, considering himself responsible before the Father for Mary and for the Child that she is carrying.

3. Joseph and the Nativity in Bethlehem

Joseph assumed the responsibility of setting off for Bethlehem with Mary who is expecting her Son, in order to obey the decree of Caesar Augustus which ordered "a census to be taken of the entire world." Luke tells us:

> And Joseph also went up from Galilee, from the city of Nazareth, to Judea, to the city of David, which is called Bethlehem, because he was of the house and lineage of David, to be enrolled with Mary, his betrothed, who was with child.
>
> And while they were there, the time came for her to be delivered. And she gave birth to her firstborn son and wrapped Him in swaddling cloths, and laid Him in a manger, because there was no place for them in the inn.[29]

The decree from Caesar Augustus is inflexible. Joseph knows

it and he obeys, in spite of Mary's condition. God makes use of this decree to ask of Joseph a new poverty for Mary's sake: she will not be able to bring her Son into the world at home in Nazareth, in a family environment; it is necessary that she accept to give birth to Him in Bethlehem, in the city of their ancestors— the city of David.

Joseph knows what a sacrifice and what a poverty this is for a young mother. He bears it all with Mary, and they will be all the more united given that nothing other than their mutual love will be the milieu that will welcome their son, the Son of God. This external poverty will be the guardian of a more intimate personal relationship.

Not only does Joseph have to accept this departure for Nazareth at a time that is so critical and so important for Mary, but he must also accept that there is no room for her at the inn in Bethlehem. The descendants of David, his own relatives, do not have enough love, enough fraternal charity, to respect Mary and to welcome her in the condition that she is in; they remain closed in their selfishness. Does not the vision in the Book of Revelation, which portrays the fury of the Dragon before the Woman who is about to give birth,[30] shed a divine light on this attitude of David's descendants in Bethlehem towards Mary, who is about to give birth? Joseph, who is responsible for Mary before the Father, endures this lack of concern and this lack of love in sorrow. He offers his pain up to the Father, and through his attention and care for Mary he makes reparation for the indifference of David's descendants.

This indifference, coming from the very people who should have been the first witnesses of this mystery which fulfills the promise made to their forefathers—this indifference allowed by God—becomes the occasion for a new intimacy between Joseph and Mary. Indeed, it is thanks to this indifference that Joseph is left alone with Mary and that, with her, he is the only witness of the mystery of the birth of God-made-man. Alone with Mary, he lives the mystery of this entirely new presence of the Son of God giving Himself to them: the *Emmanuel*, "God with us,"[31] God present for them, Yahweh the "Lord of Hosts"[32] Who disarms Himself and gives Himself as a tiny child is given to his mother.

Having witnessed Mary's divine self-abandonment during the time she was expecting her Child, Joseph now witnesses her miraculous motherhood and the first actions performed by the Mother for her Son: "She gave birth to her firstborn son and wrapped Him in swaddling clothes, and laid Him in a manger." Joseph lives together with Mary this silent, maternal liturgy of the first Christmas. He is there to safeguard her freedom as a mother; it is here that we find his silent authority at the service of these first initiatives, both motherly and liturgical. With Mary, he adores her Son, his praise joining hers. With her he lives in the silence of the tiny Child, this infant Who does not speak (*in-fans*).[33]

In a spirit of fraternal charity Joseph welcomes the shepherds—the envoys of Heaven who come "in haste" to find the "infant lying in the manger," together with Mary and Joseph.[34] With Mary, he receives their message and is amazed by all that they recount. In the depths of his heart he sings with the shepherds the song of the angels: "Glory to God in the Highest, and peace on earth among men with Whom He is pleased!"[35] How sweet and consoling for Joseph is this visit from the shepherds! It is God Himself, confirming through them, that everything that happened in the stable was indeed according to His will. The Father is pleased to see His beloved Son as a newborn child wrapped in swaddling clothes and lying in a manger, totally surrendered to Mary's love and tenderness. Joseph's greatest joy is in recognizing this. He has such admiration for Mary, and for her actions and her initiatives, that his heart is overflowing with joy in the knowledge that the Father Himself is happy with His little daughter and that all His favor rests on her. This is truly what fills Joseph's heart with the full joy of Christmas, and it is thanks to the shepherds' visit and to their message that this joy in Joseph's heart is able to blossom fully— the joy of the presence of "his" son, Who is the beloved Son of the Father, and the joy of the active presence of Mary.

4. "And at the end of eight days, when He was circumcised, He was called Jesus, the name given by the angel before He was conceived in the womb" (Luke 2:21)

According to Matthew, it is Joseph who, in obedience to the message of the angel, gives his son the name "Jesus."[36] According to Luke, it is Mary—also in obedience to the message of the angel. This is therefore their first shared task, carried out in obedience to the message of God. It is a task in which they share the exercise of their authority as father and mother, an authority exercised in a spirit of poverty, since they themselves did not choose the name for their son: it is given to them. Thus, in their shared obedience, they carry out this task together.

We must add that their obedience to the Law in having the Child circumcised is equally a part of this first shared task. In order for Jesus to make His official entrance into the religious community of Israel, their parental cooperation is necessary. They could of course have maintained that Jesus was above this requirement of the Law, this sign of the Covenant with Abraham and all his descendants. However, they understood that it was necessary to be subject to the Law and that Jesus Himself should be subject to it in order to remain hidden from the eyes of men, from the eyes of His people, and that, even more profoundly, He should be subject to the Law in order to fulfill it by living it. By being circumcised Himself, Jesus gives an entirely new value to this sign, this "sacrament"; for all Jesus' flesh, which is the flesh of the beloved Son of the Father, is entirely consecrated to God, even before He is circumcised. This sign adds nothing to Jesus, but by receiving it He gives it a new meaning.

5. The Presentation of Jesus in the Temple

The second task that Joseph and Mary share on behalf of the infant Jesus is once again a religious task, a fulfillment of the Law:

> And when the time came for their purification according to the law of Moses, they brought Him up to Jerusalem to present Him to the Lord ... and to offer a sacrifice according to what is said in the law of the Lord, "a pair of turtledoves or two young pigeons."[37]

Luke continues: "when the parents brought in the child Jesus to do for Him according to the custom of the law," the old man Simeon "inspired by the Spirit," came into the Temple, took the child up in his arms and blessed God, proclaiming that the time of waiting was over:

> Lord, now lettest Thou Thy servant depart in peace, according to Thy word, for mine eyes have seen Thy salvation, which Thou hast prepared in the presence of all peoples, a light for revelation to the Gentiles, and for glory to Thy people Israel.[38]

"And His father and mother marveled at what was said about Him," adds the Evangelist.[39] Joseph, with Mary, is filled with wonder at the prophecy of Simeon concerning the Child Jesus. Whereas Joseph had had his own annunciation, after Mary's, in which the angel had announced to him Jesus' role as the Savior of His people—saving them from their sins—this new annunciation is jointly received by Joseph and Mary, and it confirms and divinely sanctions the greatness of their common task. Simeon, in the presence of Jesus, acknowledges that the Levitic priesthood can now disappear, for it is in Jesus that the promise is fulfilled. He proclaims also that the salvation brought by Jesus is not for His people alone, but for all peoples. As the glory of Israel, Jesus is truly the light that will enlighten all the nations.

This prophecy, pronounced by Simeon the priest[40] in the presence of both Mary and Joseph, must have deeply moved Joseph, for this is the first time that they experience together and receive simultaneously a prophecy concerning Jesus, and this happens in the Temple. This prophecy announces that the old servant must disappear in order to fully make way for Jesus.

It is for Joseph and Mary—for them both—that Simeon proclaims his joy. Yet afterwards, having blessed them both, he looks at Mary alone and reveals to her:

> Behold, this child is set for the fall and rising of many in Israel, and for a sign that is spoken against (and a sword will pierce through your own soul also) that the thoughts out of many hearts may be revealed.[41]

Joseph is a witness to this prophecy concerning the Child and His Mother. He receives it in his heart, for if it is for Mary it is also for him. He must make use of this prophecy, not only to see Mary in a new light, but also to live with her the same mystery and to see Jesus in the same way that she does.

Joseph Receives a Forewarning of the Cross

Thanks to this prophecy, Joseph discovers that Mary is intimately bound to her Son in His mission: the mother must live what the Son must live. If the Son is to be "a sign that will be spoken against," she herself must accept that a sword—the sword of the Father's will for His Son—pierce her own soul.

From now on Joseph looks upon her with an even greater love, discovering her greater vulnerability, for through this prophecy he is forewarned of all that she will suffer. Without knowing the details of her sufferings, he has a foreboding of their intensity and depth. He lives in a prophetic way all that she will live at the Cross, and he accepts this mysterious will of the Father. Mary is given to him, but she belongs first of all to the Father and to His Son. Once again, he understands that he must guard her in a spirit of poverty, without having any right over her, yet loving her with an even greater strength and greater tenderness, loving her under the influence of the Holy Spirit and with His infinite sweetness. Joseph discovers here how much the Spirit loves Mary and how much the Father wishes to unite her to the mission of His Son; thus he also discovers how much the Spirit must enlarge her heart in order for it to be capable of receiving all those whom her Son will save. Joseph is forewarned of Mary's future mission which will begin later at the Cross, and, as the spouse of Mary's heart, he is to live it in a prophetic way.

6. The First Fulfillment of the Prophecy: after the Visit of the Magi, the Flight into Egypt and the Slaughter of the Innocents

Matthew recounts the visit of the Magi to Bethlehem after their having passed through Jerusalem, where their enquiries about the place where "the king of the Jews" was to be born stir up the emotions of Herod and of all Jerusalem with him. They receive the answer to their question from the scribes, who found it in the prophet Micah.[42] Having arrived in Bethlehem, "going into the house they saw the child with Mary His mother and they fell down and worshipped Him. Then, opening their treasures, they offered Him gifts, gold and frankincense and myrrh."[43] Joseph witnesses the conduct of the Magi towards the Child. This must surely have been a powerful confirmation for him of what the angel had announced to him, and also of what the shepherds had said to him. The Magi—these men from the East, these men so respectable and wise in the eyes of the world—have made this long journey in order to come and prostrate themselves before "the child," this tiny baby Who is not like other children; after Mary, Joseph knows this better than anyone. It is not the religious authorities in Jerusalem who come to prostrate themselves before Him, even though they had been alerted to His presence; no, it is these wise men from the East. Just as the shepherds took precedence over the descendants of David, so too do the Magi take precedence over the religious authorities in Jerusalem. Is this not a manifestation for Joseph, just and upright man that he is, of the order of Divine Wisdom? The poor and the little come before the self-satisfied; the shepherds and the Magi are indeed the poor, the little ones, the humble, the "hungry." Is this not what Mary had prophesied in her *Magnificat*?: "He has scattered the proud of heart, He has put down the mighty from their thrones, and exalted the lowly; He has filled the hungry with good things and the rich He has sent empty away."[44] Joseph witnesses the first fulfillment of this prophecy; and in his heart as husband and father, it is wonderful for him to experience this guiding action of God, to experience the dawn of the New Covenant. And is this not also the first fulfillment of the prophecy of the old man Simeon: "a light to enlighten the Gentiles"?

The Flight into Egypt

After the departure of the Magi, Matthew relates that:

> ... an angel of the Lord appeared to Joseph in a dream and said, "Rise, take the child and His mother, and flee to Egypt, and remain there until I tell you; for Herod is about to search for the child, to destroy Him."

> And he rose and took the child and His mother by night, and departed to Egypt, and remained there until the death of Herod.[45]

This time it is Joseph who is directly and exclusively warned by the angel. For he is indeed the visible temporal authority over Mary and Jesus—the one who is responsible at the social and political level. It is he who must make the weighty decision to leave immediately for Egypt in order to save the life of the Child Jesus by avoiding Herod's wrath. Joseph makes this decision alone, in obedience to the messenger of God. Mary has only to obey Joseph's command and carry it out "by night" with love and docility. This command is imperative—it concerns the life of the Child—and demands a total abandonment. This command appears all the more forceful, coming as it does just after the visit of the Magi when all was joy, peace and even glory. This is truly the first fulfillment of Simeon's prophecy: Jesus is "a sign that will be spoken against," and "a sword...pierce[s] the soul" of Mary.

However, this hurried departure and imposed exodus remains a joyful occasion for Joseph and Mary since they are setting off together. The Holy Family lives this time of exodus in peace and unity. It is even an opportunity for them to experience a new unity, one that is deeper, more intimate and more personal. Their first exodus was in the direction of Bethlehem, the city of their forefathers; the second is towards Egypt, the land of plenty, of seduction, and also of interior and spiritual slavery. Now, when people have to live in a foreign land, foreign in every respect, they must necessarily tighten their bonds of personal love in order to remain free from contamination, and, furthermore, they must live in a greater state of poverty and be more dependent upon others. Joseph must have known such a dependency. He was not able to provide immediately for his family from his own work; he had to accept being a foreigner, and accept it for himself, for

Mary and for Jesus. The Lord asks him to accept this poverty, to accept being stripped of everything; for a working man, this is surely the hardest kind of poverty—sacrificing the joy of being the father who works to feed his household. God really wants Joseph to be the poorest of all fathers; this allows him to be the father who is embraced most fully by the Father's mercy. From this time onwards it is through this new mercy of the Father that he loves Jesus and Mary and that he loves them even more than before.

The Slaughter of the Innocents

To this personal suffering—a suffering entirely Joseph's own but which Mary lives with him, helping and supporting him—is added another, more mysterious suffering:

> Then Herod, when he saw that he had been tricked by the wise men, was in a furious rage, and he sent and killed all the male children in Bethlehem and in all that region who were two years old and under, according to the time that he had ascertained from the wise men. Then was fulfilled what was spoken by the prophet Jeremiah: "A voice was heard in Ramah, wailing and loud lamentation, Rachel weeping for her children; she refused to be consoled, because they were no more."[46]

Responding to the call of the angel of God rather than to Herod's invitation, the Magi return home "by another route" and are the cause of Herod's bloodthirsty rage and his massacre of the "innocents," whose only crime is that of being born at the same time as Jesus and of living in or near the same city. This massacre must have been a terrifying burden for the hearts of Joseph and Mary. This is the first fruit, for His own people, of the coming of the Messiah, of the arrival on earth of the Son of the Most High! From the human perspective it is incomprehensible. Is not the massacre of one single innocent a scandal? Joseph and Mary, already filled with *Christian* faith and hope, offer all this to the

Father, without understanding its meaning. This event is indeed the "sword" for them. Mary takes the suffering of these mothers into her heart and makes it her own.

Why does God allow such injustices at the very moment when the "Prince of peace"[47] comes to "visit us"?[48] Joseph and Mary are powerless as they witness this injustice—an injustice in which they are so closely implicated: it is because of their own Child that the other children are slaughtered. This injustice, which causes so much suffering, breaks their hearts. It is harder, is it not, to bear an injustice that touches those weaker than ourselves than to bear one that touches us directly?

Joseph and Mary bear this suffering together, and it unites them further, since they must endure together the "sword" of the Father's will. They also thank God together for having spared their Child and for having saved Him from Herod's wrath.

This first communal life in Egypt together is thus lived in extreme poverty, and also in a very hidden way, for they must avoid arousing Herod's wrath once again. Joseph and Mary live this time of waiting in the abandonment of those who are poor and without defense.

7. The Return to Nazareth

But when Herod died, behold, an angel of the Lord appeared in a dream to Joseph in Egypt, saying, "Rise, take the child and His mother and go to the land of Israel, for those who sought the child's life are dead." And he rose and took the child and His mother, and went to the land of Israel. But when he heard that Archelaus reigned over Judea in place of his father Herod, he was afraid to go there, and being warned in a dream, he withdrew to the district of Galilee. And he went and dwelt in a city called Nazareth, that what was spoken through the prophets might be fulfilled, "He shall be called a Nazarene."[49]

Such is Matthew's account of the return to Nazareth. Luke says:

> And when they had performed everything according to the Law of the Lord, they returned into Galilee, to their own city, Nazareth. And the child grew and became strong, filled with wisdom; and the favor of God was upon Him.[50]

We shall not go into the historical significance of these two texts which differ in so many ways. Let us rather try to understand what they teach us about the mystery of Joseph.

Joseph's Obedience

Just as it was Joseph (according to Matthew) who assumed the responsibility for setting off to Egypt, so too does Joseph assume the responsibility for returning to the land of Israel—to Nazareth in Galilee, to be precise. Once again, Joseph makes his decision after receiving a message in a dream, and he acts in obedience to God's messenger. Matthew reveals to us through this event Joseph's complete docility to the will of God; he exercises his authority in total obedience to God's messenger, which is indeed the most divine way of exercising authority and the most contemplative way. Indeed, to exercise authority in such a way is to exercise it no longer according to our own prudence but according to God's desires, according to the order of His wisdom. When Joseph exercises his authority he does so as a contemplative. He exercises his authority in a personal union with the will of the Father. What matters to him is not what *he* wants but rather what God wants. Of course, this requires from him great poverty; it requires him to be stripped of everything. However, it is clear that whoever is to exercise authority over Mary and the Child Jesus could only exercise it in this way.

The Hidden Life

Luke speaks about the period of the "hidden life" in Nazareth during which Jesus "grew, became strong, and was filled with wisdom" under the watchful eyes of Mary and Joseph. Mary must have exercised her role as Jesus' mother during these early days of the hidden life, staying close to Him, just like all mothers, so as to bring Him up, to teach Him and to give Him His first education. This is why Luke emphasizes that Jesus "grew" and "was filled with wisdom." Jesus grew both physically and in terms of experience, even though He already enjoyed the fullness of grace in the depths of His soul and so could not really receive an education nor acquire virtues. In spite of this, Mary was to do everything for Him as if she really did have to educate Him, so as to obey the will of the Father, knowing all the while in the depths of her heart that Jesus was "holy" since He was the Son of God, for the angel Gabriel had told her so. If education is an essential part of motherhood, then Mary had to educate her Son in order to live a perfect motherhood, and yet she did so in a spirit of poverty, for a creature can have no authority over God.

In so far as education is the common task of mother and father, Joseph too participated in this task and must have performed his role, like Mary, in a spirit of poverty.

These first years in Nazareth, with the Child Jesus living so close to His mother, and Joseph working to provide the daily bread for Mary and Jesus, must have been joyful years of peace and contemplation. Joseph's work as a craftsman allowed him to remain close to Jesus and Mary, and he lived for them alone, filled with the desire to love them more and more and to know them more intimately. In the evenings, Mary must have told Joseph about everything she had lived that day with Jesus and all that Jesus was for her.

The simplicity of their life in Nazareth was matched only by the intensity and depth of the personal bonds which united all three of them. It was a true school of holiness and love. Jesus, by His silence and His example, drew the hearts of Mary and Joseph ever closer to Himself. In this community there was indeed but a single heart and a single soul.[51] Each year, Joseph and Mary traveled to Jerusalem for the Passover festival.[52] In the depths of their hearts and in an intimate way, they were living a Christian life, yet they remained living members of the People of Israel, perfectly observing the precepts of the Law and enjoying this trip to Jerusalem for the Passover.

8. Jesus, at the age of twelve, teaches the Doctors in the Temple

And when He was twelve years old, they went up [to Jerusalem] according to custom [for the feast of the Passover]; and when the feast was ended, as they were returning, the boy Jesus stayed behind in Jerusalem. His parents did not know it, but supposing Him to be in the company, they went a day's journey and they sought Him among their kinsfolk and acquaintances; and when they did not find Him, they returned to Jerusalem, seeking Him. After three days they found Him in the temple, sitting among the teachers, listening to them and asking them questions; and all who heard Him were amazed at His understanding and His answers.[53]

Jesus is now twelve years old. The first period of His education, received from His mother, has now come to an end. This is the first time that He travels up to Jerusalem with His parents to celebrate the feast of the Passover with them. This is without doubt a great joy for Mary and Joseph, who love their religion very much. As they pray, worship and praise God in the Temple, accompanied by Jesus and praying with Him, they also contemplate Jesus praying in the Temple with all His people. No one has ever prayed as He prayed, but no one notices Him because His prayer is so simple and profound and entirely for God.

It is in this profound joy that they leave Jerusalem, untroubled in any way. Yet Jesus, without a word of warning, stays behind in Jerusalem to give the first fruits of His teaching ministry to the doctors of the Law. As an intelligent child is wont to do, He asks them questions, for this is the most merciful way to teach. Jesus knows that if He teaches them in this way, they will listen to Him, whereas later, when He teaches with authority at the age of thirty, they will no longer listen to Him (with the exception of Nicodemus). Luke emphasizes that "All those who heard Him were amazed at His understanding and His answers." At twelve years of age, Jesus wants to help these doctors of the Law to have a deeper understanding of Scripture. He wants to help them to have a more divine faith. He uses the Word of God to compel them to enter more deeply into the mystery, to go further in searching for the truth.

Joseph's Anguish

While Jesus is sitting amidst the doctors in the Temple, Mary and Joseph are beset with worry and anguish, not knowing where to find Him. They have lost every trace of His presence. Jesus could have spared them this suffering by letting them know beforehand. They would surely have agreed and even understood this priestly haste of Christ, this haste to be a witness to the truth.[54] Yet Jesus has not told them anything, even though He knew how much suffering this would cause them. It is He Himself Who drives the sword into their hearts, and He must do so, for He is the One sent by the Father, the One Who is entirely "about [His] Father's affairs."

This suffering, this sadness, this agony in the hearts of Joseph and Mary, of which He is the cause, has a deep and mysterious meaning, which Joseph and Mary do not understand at the time; their lack of comprehension is moreover an essential part of this mystery. Agony is only agony when we cannot see the sense of it, when it is utterly dark and impenetrable. Is not this suffering, this sadness, this agony, willed by God so that Joseph and Mary might cooperate in their own way in the beginning of Jesus' teaching ministry and in the first moments of His apostolic life? Is this not the second fulfillment of the prophecy of the old Simeon? There is no doubt that the sword penetrates Mary's heart the most deeply, but it pierces Joseph's as well. In their common suffering, in their shared sadness and anguish, Joseph and Mary come to know a new degree of intimacy; together they bear the first fruits of Jesus' apostolic life. They have not found themselves alone together, face-to-face in this way, since the first moment when they met. And here they are alone together, bearing their shared suffering: the absence of Jesus—an unbearable, incomprehensible absence. It is still Jesus Who unites them, yet now He does so by His absence, through a foreshadowing of His Cross, of the mission given to Him by the Father.

Thus, during these three days, Joseph and Mary come to know a profound unity in their suffering, a new mutual confidence. Joseph suffers not only because of the absence of Jesus but also because of the suffering that this absence causes in Mary's heart. He bears these two sufferings, this double sword which is but one, and which, because of Mary's suffering, has a particular sharpness for Joseph's heart. Mary herself suffers firstly on account of Jesus' absence, but she also suffers on Joseph's account; Joseph's sadness is unbearable for her: he really does not deserve this! This man so just and so righteous should not know such anguish. Why did Jesus behave like this? He is normally so docile and obedient, so wonderfully good and respectful of Joseph's authority. Why this sudden incomprehensible behavior? And for Mary, who is so close to her Jesus, so intimately united to Him—He is her beloved Son with Whom she is "well pleased"—why this silence, this estrangement? Why this new attitude suddenly, without a word of explanation?

Mary may well have asked herself all these questions out of love for Joseph, fearing that he himself would be asking questions of this sort. But, in fact, she surrenders herself—in suffering and in sorrow, accepting not to understand—to the Father's gracious will. Love remains present in her heart, a love full of suffering, grief and anguish, but a love which is victorious over everything. In this trial, Mary is Joseph's strength and hope; she is his light. Thanks to her, Joseph can endure this trial with love. They both suffer a real interior martyrdom during the course of these three days, indeed a *true* martyrdom, since it is endured in love. Their souls remain totally surrendered to the gracious will of the Father, begging Him to be there to help them in their searching, lest they waste any time.

Why have You done this to us?

Finding Him three days later, sitting in the Temple in the midst of the teachers and asking them questions,

> …when they saw Him they were astonished; and His mother said to Him, "Son, why have You done this to us? Behold, Your father and I have been looking for You anxiously."[55]

It is Mary who expresses her astonishment to Jesus, an astonishment which is almost a reproach, "Why have You done this to us?" And to emphasize the significance of Jesus' action, she points out its consequences: the anxiety of Joseph, His father, and her own suffering united to Joseph's. This is the first and indeed the only time that Mary calls Joseph His "father" when speaking to Jesus about Joseph. She truly considers him as Jesus' father, since he is her spouse.

This is also the first and only time that we see Mary asking Jesus a question—asking Him why He acted as He did. This shows us just how bewildered Mary must have been: it would seem that she cannot bear any more grief, probably because of

Joseph's dismay and anguish. It is so difficult for this just and righteous man to live such a sudden, unusual, irrational and incomprehensible event! Mary has to support Joseph in his dismay; she has to wed herself to him in her heart. Had she been alone, she would probably have kept silent and not said anything. But Joseph is there too, and he would not have understood her silence, for he is undoubtedly the more desolate of the two and the one who suffers the most anguish. He suffers as a just man, and as a man who loves Mary and who cannot bear to see her suffering; he suffers also as a father, no longer understanding where his responsibility for Jesus lies or how he should exercise it.

Mary and Joseph, two people who love each other very deeply, live this painful event by helping each other and supporting each other, but they are also a source of suffering for each other: Mary's cross is carried by Joseph, and Joseph's cross is carried by Mary. Father and mother each have their cross. By carrying each other's cross, they help each other, but they are also the source of new sufferings for one another. It is thus that we can understand Mary's question to Jesus, which is perhaps more of a prayer than a question—a prayer for Joseph: "Son, why have You done this to us? Behold *Your father* and I have been looking for You anxiously..." In her humility she allies herself to Joseph; whatever Joseph lives, she is to live as well.

Why were you looking for Me?

Jesus' reply remains a great mystery: "Why were you looking for Me? Did you not know that I must be about My Father's affairs?" But, adds Luke, "they did not understand the saying which He spoke to them."[56]

Jesus' reply is not that of a child. Mary's question was addressed to her child and to Joseph's child. Jesus replies as the One sent by the Father "Who is in Heaven." By staying behind with the doctors without warning Mary and Joseph, He acted not as their child, but as the One sent by the Father, as One Who has a divine mission to accomplish. Indeed, He has just accomplished the first fulfillment of His mission, and this is why He acted as He did: so that Mary and Joseph might understand His radical and total dependence on His Father. He is subject to Mary and to Joseph only in so far as the Father wishes Him to be. They only have such authority as the Father delegates to them, and in His teaching ministry and His apostolic life He is solely dependent upon the Father. This is His priestly mission, which He accomplishes as the Envoy of the Father, and it is right that His teaching is reserved for the doctors of the People of Israel.

If we interpret Jesus' words, are we to say that He intended to correct His parents by reminding them that they ought to have understood His attitude, since He had come into the world to accomplish the will of His Father? No, He is not reproaching them. He is calling them to rise above their present state, by placing a new demand before them, by asking a new poverty of them. Do we not see here the first time that Jesus looks upon His parents and speaks to them as Priest, as the One sent by the Father? This is what is completely new here. A new stage has begun in His life; His parents are to understand this, and this is why they should no longer look on Him as a child: He is now wholly given over to His Father's affairs.

We can understand that in order to live this Mary and Joseph must die spiritually in their roles as father and mother. This is indeed what the Evangelist highlights, "They did not understand the saying that He spoke to them." They have to accept in their hearts that Jesus will go ahead of them and that He will fully accomplish the Father's will.

9. The Second Period of the Hidden Life

And He went down with them and came to Nazareth, and was obedient to them; and His mother kept all these things in her heart. And Jesus increased in wisdom and in stature, and in favor with God and man.[57]

Since Jesus' depth of understanding amazed the teachers of Israel, should He not have stayed in Jerusalem and entered the rabbinical school? No, He returns to Nazareth with Joseph and Mary and continues to live as an obedient son. What is new in this second period of the hidden life is that Jesus is taught by Joseph, His father, to learn His trade and to be a craftsman with him—to become a carpenter. This time He is truly educated directly by Joseph and comes to know, through this experience, a new closeness with him. Luke emphasizes that He "was obedient to them." Furthermore, from this point onwards, Jesus reads the Scriptures with Mary and Joseph and teaches them to read the Scriptures by listening to His parents and asking them questions, just as He had done with the doctors in the Temple. With this teaching, the first exercise of His priesthood is for Mary and Joseph. Luke tells us, "And His mother kept all these things in her heart."

There are two aspects here that we should keep in mind (Luke emphasizes them), two kinds of docility: the docility of Jesus' heart, as He is taught by Joseph, and the docility of Mary's heart. Joseph is filled with joy to witness the profound docility present in the hearts of Jesus and Mary, and to witness, in this atmosphere of docility, Jesus' growth "in wisdom and in stature and in favor."

This second period of life in Nazareth is, like the first, a period of contemplation. Yet it differs from the first in that Jesus must increasingly exercise, for Mary and Joseph, His prophetic teaching ministry—reading the Word of God and explaining the prophets—

and He must live, with them and for them, His life of adoration and praise, His life of work and fraternal charity. We know nothing of this life, so rich in the eyes of God and so hidden from the eyes of men.

10. Joseph's Departure

Neither Scripture nor Tradition says anything to us about the end of Joseph's earthly life in Nazareth: we have no words about it either from Mary or Jesus. All the signs would suggest that Joseph had disappeared from the scene by the time of Jesus' departure for the desert—a departure which marks the beginning of His apostolic life—since Mary seems to be on her own at Cana and begins to follow Jesus from then on.[58]

This silence in both Scripture and Tradition concerning the end of Joseph's earthly pilgrimage is very meaningful; this father who is so poor leaves as a legacy this silence and this departure in obedience to the Father's will. Joseph never looks upon himself with self-satisfaction: his only desire is to accomplish the Father's will through the exercise of his authority over Jesus and Mary. He disappears when God asks him to do so. Having always been a servant who is poor in spirit, he joyfully steps aside to leave Mary alone with her Son; now that his temporal function is completed, all that remains for him is to disappear. Yet even after his departure he remains present within the Holy Family, in the hearts of Jesus and Mary.

We cannot help but admire the stark simplicity and poverty of Joseph's end. We know where the patriarchs were buried: Scripture tells us the resting places of Abraham, Isaac and Jacob. Throughout every generation their descendants would come to the place of their burial, at Hebron or Shechem. We are told nothing about Joseph: no trace of him remains on earth. On account of this silence some claim that he was taken up into

Heaven. Yet we can interpret this silence in a different way and understand that it helps us to discover Joseph's spiritual poverty—the poverty of this father who exercised so unique an authority and who is truly the servant *par excellence*—the servant of the New Covenant, gentle and faithful but dispensable.[59] Surely, is not the greatest legacy left to us by this dispensable servant the very fact that no trace remains of him?

Joseph is a "son of David," like Solomon. They are both endowed with an outstanding divine wisdom, and they are both appointed to be guardians of the Temple of God. However, unlike Solomon, who became a "slave to his senses"[60] because of his excessive love for women—so much so that "his heart was not wholly true to the Lord" and "he did not wholly follow the Lord as David his father had done"[61]—Joseph loves Mary alone and his heart remains wholly true to the Lord, and he obeys Him even more perfectly than his father David did. Solomon was buried "in the city of David,"[62] but, once again, we are told nothing of Joseph's burial. His name disappears; it "ends in God"[63]—in the Son of God.

11. Joseph, Spouse of Mary

The mysterious greatness of Joseph within the Divine Economy lies in the fact that he is truly Mary's spouse and, for this reason, Jesus' father. When Joseph freely chose Mary to be his wife (for this was his heart's first intention), he had to accept that this choice would be accomplished according to God's will for Mary, since Mary had already offered herself entirely to her God. This is the radical purification that God demands of Joseph's heart. His love for Mary must be offered to the Father and is only to be fulfilled in accordance with God's will.

Surely this is what God demands of every human love: that it be supernaturalized through charity, and radically so. However, in Joseph's case, that which ordinarily is radical and fundamental becomes explicit and present "in act." In order for him to espouse Mary in truth, he has to live in his heart what she herself lives in relation to her God: the offering of one's entire life in total surrender.

Guardian of the Virgin

This requirement demands that his love as a spouse, the love he lives in his heart as a man, be sacrificed to God, so that charity can take hold of everything and become the more significant love. His love as a husband has to be radically impoverished. He becomes the guardian of the Virgin—he who bears the responsibility of keeping her hidden by taking her into his home and entering into such a closeness with her, so as to be docile to the will of the Father with her. Joseph must become a virginal husband if he is to espouse the Virgin who is consecrated to God. He truly espouses her by becoming her guardian, he who officially takes her into his home, and he does so in order to offer her personally and intimately to God, to the Father. This is a free choice made in deep poverty, in the acceptation of not possessing her who, being wholly given to God, gives herself to him so that he will watch over her, loving her *as she is*, that is to say, wholly given to God.

Thanks to Joseph and to Joseph's love for her, Mary can give herself even more to God, since she gives herself to God in offering to Him Joseph's love for her.

God takes Mary at her word when she abandons herself to His will: He asks her if she will agree to be the mother of the "Son of the Most High." He does so without asking Joseph's opinion, since Mary had already given herself totally to Him before she was entrusted to Joseph. In becoming the Mother of God, through her *fiat* and through the direct and immediate working of the Holy Spirit, Mary continues to remain wholly and immediately dependent upon the Father's gracious will.

There is no radical change within her heart, but God takes over her life in such a way that she becomes the Mother of God, and she freely accepts this. Joseph has some idea of what is happening within her, but, not being able to understand it and fearing himself to be an obstacle to the workings of God within Mary, he decides to distance himself from her, to send her back home and to let her be free. But God wants Joseph to receive her once again with a new love, with a love that is poorer and more trusting. The fact that God has drawn Mary into a greater personal intimacy by making her the Mother of His beloved Son does not mean that Joseph must withdraw as if he were excluded. Quite the contrary, the more God draws a creature to Himself the more capable that creature becomes of loving those whom God brings close to him or her; thus Mary becomes more able to welcome Joseph, to love him, and to give herself to him. God is not the rival of human love, but when His love is communicated to His creatures it requires their human love to become truer, purer and poorer.

Joseph is to love Mary as a husband loves his wife and with the same intensity of love, yet he lives this love without having any claim on her. She belongs to God even more than before since she is the Mother of the Son of God. It is in poverty that love can blossom and intensify. Joseph is glad that the Father is well-pleased with Mary, and he loves her all the more because God has bestowed His affection on her. God's affection for Mary does not exclude Joseph's affection for her. On the contrary, God's affection, which comes first, calls forth Joseph's own affection.

Father of the Child

In taking Mary—who bears the Son of God—into his home, and in taking her to be his wife, Joseph becomes the father of Him Whom she is carrying. Like his spousal love, this fatherhood can only be exercised in extreme poverty and without any consequent rights, since, like his spousal love, his fatherhood is deprived of its natural biological basis. The whole aspect of sexuality is completely transcended so that there is nothing but a personal divine love that assumes their spiritual and sensible[64] human love in a unique way. The bonds that unite the hearts of Joseph and Mary are of an amazing clarity and strength. It really is a total and personal gift of self that they make to each other, under the motion of the Holy Spirit—a gift which prolongs the gift that each one has made to God, one gift intensifying and revealing the other, even as it hides it. This personal gift of self goes so far as to include their individual sensibilities, which become harmonized and united.

The bonds that exist between the heart of Joseph and that of the Child Jesus are—since Jesus is God—of an even more amazing clarity and strength. No child has ever been so united to his father as Jesus is to Joseph; no father has ever been so united to his child as Joseph is to Jesus. Joseph loves Jesus' heart—a heart so burning with love, so humble, so poor and so gentle; he loves it with a divine love, which is "substantial" and eternal. He is wholly given to Jesus and loves Him with all his heart as a man and as a father, and with all his sensibility, for Joseph loves the sensibility of Jesus' heart, which is so close to Mary's heart.

Faithful Servant, Instrument of the Father

Thanks to this love that is so strong, so intense and so absolute, Joseph will be the servant *par excellence* of Jesus and Mary—a gentle and faithful servant who is poor in spirit. His service is the temporal authority that he is to exercise over Mary and Jesus. He performs this service with gentleness, faithfulness and poverty, for he performs it in profound docility to the Father's authority; it is the Father's gracious will that he seeks above all else. He performs this service with a total clarity of heart, giving himself and offering all his strength and energy, without seeking any pleasure for himself and without a trace of selfishness in seeking his own personal preferences. He performs this service in a true spirit of poverty, knowing that it is the Father Who is working through him. He seeks to be His instrument, with more concern for the Father's wishes than for the work he himself is accomplishing.

By exercising this authority at the temporal level in service to Mary and Jesus, Joseph is the Father's instrument. He does not exercise a priestly authority. He is truly the instrument of the Father, and it is the Father's authority that he represents and exercises. Priestly authority is the Father's authority present in His beloved Son. As for Mary, she exercises no authority other than the moral authority of a mother—an authority which, transformed by charity and infused prudence, is in fact a participation both in the priesthood of Christ and in the maternal authority of the Holy Spirit. (Mary's Christian grace means that she participates in Christ's priesthood, and it allows her to be intimately associated with the work of the Holy Spirit.)

12. The Royal Priesthood of Joseph

It is important to understand that the Holy Family is the foundation of the Church. Is the Holy Family really not the only "foundational community" of the Church? In this community the visible authority belongs to Joseph and it is an authority which is a service of love and mercy; it lets Jesus and Mary take precedence. In the Old Covenant, the father's authority (that of the patriarch—of Abraham) is always first, and the son's authority only comes second. In the New Covenant, however, it is the authority of the beloved Son—to Whom, precisely, the Father has given all authority—that holds first place. This authority is a priestly authority in the strongest sense, assuming both royal and prophetic authority. In the New Covenant there are, in fact, two ways of participating in this authority: there is the royal and mystical priesthood of the faithful, and there is the ministerial priesthood of the ordained priest. In the Holy Family, everything began with the royal and mystical priesthood of the Woman—Mary—to which the royal and mystical priesthood of Joseph was joined.

Let us look at the proper character of each of these two priestly participations that cooperate with the coming of Jesus into the world, with His birth and with His hidden life in our midst. Mary's priesthood is exercised in a divine motherhood that is entirely at the service of the priestly authority of Christ—as much from the mystical perspective as from the temporal one (although differently so in each case, of course). Concerning Joseph, Mary's royal priesthood is exercised in the service of Joseph's temporal authority and cooperates with his own royal priesthood in the very exercise of their mutual fraternal charity, which has the special modality of a love between husband and wife.

As for Joseph's royal priesthood,[65] he exercises it first (as we have just said) with respect to Mary: "Do not be afraid to take Mary your wife into your home"; the spousal authority which Joseph exercises over Mary is indeed a participation in the priestly authority of Christ.

In his fraternal charity towards Mary, Joseph also cooperates with her for the good of the Holy Family, and in this cooperation he listens attentively to Mary. For was he not the first one in whom she placed all her trust and whom she could even ask to be the guardian of her silence, to guard the secrets of God concerning her? This was indeed what first put the seal on Mary's trust in Joseph. Joseph cooperates with Mary through the exercise of his paternal authority over Jesus, as the one responsible for the growth of Jesus' temporal life and for the blossoming of His human life, as if it really is his duty to educate Him and to help

Him to reach adulthood. These two different exercises, namely fraternal love towards Mary and authority over Jesus, stem from Christ's priesthood and are finalized by it.

13. Joseph, Model for Deacons

Joseph thus appears as the model for all those who exercise a temporal authority in the Church that is directly and entirely at the service of Christ's priesthood, through the mediation of Mary. Is he not thus the deacon *par excellence*, as it were? It would be helpful to compare the service of Saint Stephen with that of Joseph, since they were each saints in the service that they performed, both accepting to disappear from the world so as to remain faithful and to be nothing but servants of Christ's priesthood and of the ministerial priesthood of the Apostles. Like Stephen, deacons participate in the ministerial authority of the ordained priesthood and in this way form part of the hierarchy. Joseph, however, precedes the hierarchy: he receives his authority (authority as husband over Mary and as father over Jesus) directly from the Father, through the mediation of the angel, and thus has no need to be ordained deacon! He is, then, as it were, the *archetypal* deacon (the "transcendent" model), whereas Stephen, in a different way, is the first to fill this ecclesial office. This allows us to see that Joseph, as the archetypal deacon, fulfills his office of service in the silence of contemplation, whereas Stephen, coming after him, fulfills his office as deacon through the proclamation of the Word and by "serving at table."[66] Once again, everything is founded on the silence of contemplation, which is continued in the Church with the monastic life. Thus it is that we can understand the distinctive link that exists between Saint Joseph and the monastic life.

LIVING WITH SAINT JOSEPH

Part Two of this volume is a collection of spoken lectures that complements Part One by showing how Saint Joseph sheds light on our own lives and can help us to live the Christian life fully.

1

THE WORKER

On the first of May the Church celebrates the feast of "Saint Joseph the Worker." This is indeed one of the great aspects of Saint Joseph's greatness: he who was a "son of David"[67] was a "worker" and a "servant." It is quite surprising to see that there are no sons of David among the Apostles, whereas it was necessary that there should be this son of David as the husband of the Virgin Mary, "of whom was born Jesus, Who is called the Christ."[68] A "good and faithful servant,"[69] Saint Joseph was most certainly a good worker, and he it is who teaches us to be true laborers for God—in other words, friends of God who do not see only the material, temporal aspect of what we are doing. Saint Joseph helps us to understand the greatness of work in the eyes of God.

Human work and the Spirit of the Gospel

Intellectual work and manual work are often put in opposition to each other, but this would be to look at it from a sociological perspective, not a Christian one. Many Christians today, affected by a master-slave dialectic, believe that everything that originates from the working classes must be evangelical in spirit, since the working classes are the poor people.[70] One of the great faults of our age is that we exalt the worker in opposition to the intellectual, despising the intellectual. This opposition does not come from God any more than does the contrary tendency of exalting the intellectual to the detriment of the worker or the craftsman. Let us not confuse Christianity, which, coming from the Holy Spirit (the Spirit of love), is above human conditioning, with work (that of the craftsman or the factory worker, or the intellectual work of a philosopher or a theologian), which is part of our human conditioning. A worker may be a skilled worker (either a craftsman or an intellectual) or he may be a bad worker; he may be a failure or a success; he may be gifted at his work, a prodigy; all of this remains at the human level.

To think that everything that originates with the working classes is necessarily evangelical in spirit is to confuse the human level with the supernatural, Christian level. This is as blatant a confusion as the one whereby the intellectual work carried out by a talented person is attributed to the action of the Holy Spirit. We thus see two extreme confusions, each as regrettable as the other, both of which are forms of positivism (for there is a Christian form of positivism).[70b] Like all social environments, the working classes have their strengths and their weaknesses. After all, different human circumstances bring with them different sorts of strengths, as well as the weaknesses which are the consequences of original sin. What is important is that the spirit of the Gospel lift us above all of this. As Saint Paul said, we are neither slaves nor free men, Greeks nor Jews; we are Christians, we belong to Christ.[71] The renewal of the Church desired by the Second Vatican Council powerfully reminds us that we belong to Christ, and that the "Christian" denominator is stronger than everything else. We often live this badly because we do not live it fully, but this is what every true Christian desires to live and *should* live very profoundly. It is wonderful, then, to see the victory of grace: we can go beyond our human conditioning, which all too often determines what we do. We do not deny our conditioning, of course, but it remains a conditioning factor only, and so does not determine us. Whilst it is clear that we are influenced psychologically by our early childhood and by our initial family environment, we do not live at that level. Saint Joseph is the saint who helps us to understand this.

Sanctification through Work

By not wasting time, by remaining focused on his work, by not being excitable or chatty, nor proud or possessive, Joseph performed his work with love. He thus shows us that the Church began with the sanctification of work.[72] He teaches us to make work a means for our sanctification, since through work we cooperate with the Father's will for us. Work allows us to manifest our love for the Father and our desire to glorify Him. Once again, whether our work be manual work or intellectual work is of little importance; this is not what counts in God's eyes. What is important is that we perform it in this spirit, namely, with the desire of glorifying the Father and loving Him through and in our work. It is then that work becomes something very great indeed, and we understand Jesus' words spoken the day after the multiplication of the loaves: "Do not labor for the food which perishes [for the pagan does as much] but for the food which endures to eternal life, which the Son of Man will give to you"[73]— that is to say, the Eucharist. Admittedly, Saint Joseph could not labor for the Eucharist, since this mystery had not yet been revealed to him, but he could labor to glorify the Creator by participating in His work,[74] and, furthermore, to glorify the Father by accomplishing His will. In this he anticipated what Jesus would ask of us: to offer up, through our work, the matter for sacrifice— bread and wine, "fruit of the earth [the vine] and work of human hands."[75]

Saint Joseph is not a saint because he was a good worker who knew how to work well with matter. He is the patron saint of workers because he knew how to rise above not only the concern for efficiency and the need to dominate the matter we work with but also above the joy of a job well done, in order to offer it to God. For this reason we can properly call Saint Joseph "model of love" rather than "model of work." He was indeed a tireless worker, but, for him, work was not just something that allows man to gain food and money. He did his work in the best possible way but this was not what was most important to him. He did not work in order to become a specialist, or to win a prize, or again for human glory. He worked for the sole reason that God asked him to; he worked in order to fulfill His will. Obedience to God, and the fact of being predominantly concerned with doing His will, gives gentleness to our work. We do not waste time, and we work without stress or fuss. We work ardently (with the ardor that comes from adoration) yet without agitation, and joyfully—with the joy of giving all our time to God.

As a "just and God-fearing man,"[76] Joseph knew that, since the Fall, God has asked man to work "by the sweat of [his] brow"[77] for six days of the week,[78] and that work is done in obedience to God, to do His will, to become ever more docile to His Spirit, always accepting that we do not "possess"[79] our work. We are always tempted, in fact, to seek visible success; we are tempted by the human glory of having others look at us and be interested in us, of being famous. However, if we seek the glory that comes from men,[80] then true prayer is completely lost; adoration and contemplation are completely lost. Saint Joseph helps us not to give into the temptation of human glory and any form of worldly Messianism. He keeps us from becoming drunk with success and with the reputation we have or seek to have. This is vital, for herein lies a major obstacle to the beatitude of the poor. "Fear of the Lord is the root of wisdom";[81] in other words, poverty is that without which there is no contemplation. And without interior poverty there is no longer any real divine hope.

We can be certain that Saint Joseph never wasted time[82] and that he detested dilettantism.[83] Wherever we find dilettantism, even in a pious, "baptized" form, there is no place there for Saint Joseph. He himself worked too seriously to fall into that trap. He had the seriousness of a true worker. But the seriousness of a true worker is not the same as a bad mood! On the contrary, the more serious we are about our work the more we are in a good mood. Working seriously puts all our grumpiness to flight. Work, in its realism, and in the intention with which we do it (namely, for God and in order to be united to Him by doing the will of the Father), *purifies* us. Let us not forget that Jesus did not come to *free* us from work. Work purifies us: it purifies the intelligence from all that is imaginary, which encumbers us, and it also contributes to the purification of our hearts from the imaginary, and from romanticism. It allows fraternal charity to be incarnated (we work *for* our brothers and often *with* them, in cooperation with them). He who claims to love and does not work does not really love: he remains a dilettante, a romantic. Romantic love is never incarnated—it doesn't need to be, since it is romantic! Realistic love, on the other hand, needs to be incarnated in some form of work.

The Contemplative Worker

The holiness of Saint Joseph cannot be understood only in terms of the sanctification of work. The sanctification of work is a good thing, but it derives from something else, since work comes second not first, from the human point of view. Work in itself is an activity of transformation; it concerns the "becoming," and the "becoming" is never something first. Saint Joseph's sanctification of work derives from his contemplative attitude, and the sanctification of work for us (i.e. working with a view to the mystery of the Eucharist) can only come about thanks to contemplation—to the desire for contemplation.[84] Our desire for contemplation gives us an interior freedom which allows us to work in truth and with determination, thereby making a total gift of all our strength, and offering our work to God as a holocaust of love. In order for this work to be offered up to God as a holocaust of love (if we are looking for more than just a satisfying result), we need to have a great love for God, a love so great that we seek only His will and no longer our own. If we do not have this love, it will not be possible to offer up our work as a holocaust. When work is accomplished in simply the human, natural perspective, we have a specific goal in mind, which remains on the human plane, and we become attached to our work. In religious life we discover that it takes a long time for work, and for our way of working, to become purified. It is not something that is done in a day, nor even a year; it takes a lifetime, because it is the whole reality of our human person that is involved in work—including our sensibility, our emotions (especially when we work in cooperation with another person or when our work is repetitive), our imagination, our intelligence and our will to apply ourselves to what we do. Work should normally sharpen our intelligence. When it dulls our intelligence (this is something that can happen now and again), this proves that our work is no longer what it ought to be. Work should always ennoble us; it should always allow our intelligence to go further, because it is an experience—the experience of transforming matter in order to bring creation to a certain completion, to complement and crown it.

Whether we are working towards a purely human goal or whether we are working for Jesus, this work requires intelligence—practical or speculative intelligence, depending on the nature of the work. Some days we may work badly because our intelligence is a little sleepy and does not manage to wake up fully. At times like that we feel that what we are doing is not very useful. We need to have the courage to go back to the source so that, in finding it, we can discover our capacity to work in a fully human way, and in a Christian way if we are Christian. Work should always ennoble us at the human level, and it should make us "committed" Christians as they say nowadays, that is, Christians who are capable of witnessing and who do not hesitate to do so. Because of the love that unites us to Christ and of which we are witnesses, we Christians understand that our work no longer has simply the finality of ordinary human work. This first end, namely, the final product to be accomplished, needs to be surpassed: "Work, not for perishable food" (this is the first, immediate end) "but for the bread which the Son of Man will give to you." We see that this new end is not at all of the same order as the first; it is much more profound and goes much further. And to pass from the first finality to the second, there needs to be a great love—a supernatural love, that is, charity—and it is not very easy.

Take the example of a young religious Brother attending a philosophy class (and, what's more, in the morning before breakfast!).[85] Is he doing so simply as he waits for his breakfast, or in order to become more intelligent, or in order to glorify the Father? If he is there to become more intelligent, that's good, but it is still not enough. Of course you must attend the class for that reason, but you must attend it with a view to something much more profound, namely the mystery of the Eucharist. These words of Jesus are very powerful words; they show us that work should *always* dispose us for the Eucharist, should always direct us towards the Eucharist. Work is the most common experience of our human lives. How amazed we would be if we were to count the number of hours in our lives we spend working! Any form of religious life is fundamentally a life that is an ordered life (following a rule), a hidden life and a silent life of work. As religious we can always work in a humble and poor way, stopping every so often to adore and thus renew our momentum, so that our hearts always remain turned towards God, always remain in the presence of God Who dwells within us. Work and adoration go together and are the foundation of the religious life.

Here we touch upon that aspect of work as something that glorifies the Father because it is done with love. If we live in the world then the love which binds us to Jesus and to the Father, if it is strong enough, will allow us to go beyond the satisfaction of a job well done (and well paid) to the understanding that work allows us to be associated with the will of the Father,[86] even unto the labor of the Cross. "My Father is at work until now, so I am at work."[87] The work that the Father asks Jesus to accomplish is the work of Redemption, the work of the Cross.[88] That is why, when we do it in a truly Christian way, our work allows us to offer ourselves more fully and to be more immediately in contact with the Eucharist. But this can only happen if we have within us a great love, and hence a desire for contemplation.

Worker and Father

Let us note further that Joseph is also the patron saint of workers because he enabled Mary to educate Jesus; he formed, together with her, an environment in which the Child Jesus could live, grow and become a man in the eyes of the world.[89] Joseph was a father, and we know what psychologists say about the formation of the person: inherited influences count for about forty per cent and education for about sixty per cent. That's important! (It is for this reason that we should encourage parents who cannot have children to adopt.) Saint Joseph is therefore truly a father—all the more so because it is God Himself Who came first in this fatherhood, and God is never a rival to His creatures.[90]

As a father, Joseph works in poverty because he knows that

he is not Jesus' father by flesh and blood: he accepted to receive his son from the Holy Spirit and from Mary. Yet, because this is the work of God, he welcomes the Child in a more profound way than a father of flesh and blood would have welcomed the son that his wife bore him. The work of God in Mary, combined with Joseph's poverty, make him more a father than any other human father.

If God asks Joseph for such great poverty in his work, it is so that this work may have a "divine" fruitfulness that goes well beyond the normal fruits of human labor. Even if Joseph does not work explicitly for the Eucharist, he works for the One Who will give it, Jesus. Joseph accepts to work as the father of Him Who is the Son of God. His human fatherhood, therefore, is the greatest human fatherhood that ever existed.

It is truly great to proclaim Joseph as father and model of workers right from the beginning of the Church. The Church is founded upon Joseph and Peter—they are her two foundations: on the one hand, the bread, on the other, the rock. Joseph really does represent bread, since bread is the fruit of work. The Holy Spirit uses the work of man in order to bring about the Eucharist, in other words, in order to bring the Covenant with Jesus, the Son of God to perfection.

The Work of the Cross

In today's world, people do not love their work because they no longer see its purpose, and because work today is bought and sold. Wherever the Christian is, therefore, he must be an example of the nobility and the greatness of work, and show that the New Covenant in Christ is a covenant of workers in the strongest sense, since Jesus gives us His testament by using bread and wine. Jesus could have given His "last testament" in pure divine wisdom and written it in His own hand. In that case the testament He left us would have been that of seeking the truth. "I have come to bear witness to the truth,"[91] He says to Pilate, in a magnificent testimony before a temporal power. But the testament that He leaves to His disciples is the gift of Himself. Let us never separate what God has joined together,[92] namely, being a witness to the truth and giving oneself for the labor of the Cross. The labor of the Cross is the ultimate sanctification of the human body. The human body, which is normally a source of labor, can be offered as a victim in the passivity of a total, radical love. Though no longer able to work, one can still be a victim of love. The labor of the Cross is no longer a labor that results in a finished product; it is Jesus offering His body as a victim of love.[93]

Everything is fulfilled in the Cross. Joseph experienced this when the twelve-year-old Jesus began to work by teaching the doctors in the Temple[94]—for teaching is clearly a work; it is the work of someone who wants to bear witness to the truth. However, this work is not true unless it is associated with the Cross and with the Eucharist.

Saint Joseph shows us the kind of work that God loves: a work that is humble, hidden, fervent and carried out in poverty. He works for the glory of God alone and with the greatest possible gratuity.

Through this we come to understand why Joseph has been proclaimed by the Church as the saint who is to help us discover the profound value of work. The Church could have proclaimed him the model of Christian husbands, or the model of fathers and of paternal responsibility. When she chose the title "Joseph the Worker," she did so in order to remind us of the dignity of human work[95] and of the meaning of Christian work,[96] but also to show us that Joseph's holiness is one that is profoundly incarnated. He is of course a model of love and of purity in love, a model of responsibility and prudence, but all of this is based upon a more hidden holiness: that of the worker, of a worker who had the unique privilege of working alongside, as well as *for*, the Son of God made man.

We thus discover a very fundamental and hidden aspect of Joseph's holiness. He is holy in his fidelity to his work, in the meekness which characterized his work and in the spiritual poverty of his work.[97] We need to go this far in order to understand how divine love took possession of his whole heart and sensibility, all his labor and energy. His whole person and activity was entirely sanctified by the grace that he received from Jesus and Mary.

2

SPOUSE OF MARY

If Saint Joseph is indeed the meek, faithful and poor servant,[98] and thus the model of the Christian worker, he is even more the "husband of Mary." He appears in Revelation as relative to Mary:[99] "Jacob was the father of Joseph, the husband of Mary, of whom Jesus was born, Who is called the Christ."[100]

Joseph's First Choice: Mary Consecrated to God

Joseph chose Mary, and he chose her with joy. There must have been such joy and blossoming in Joseph's heart when he discovered Mary and became certain that she had responded to his choice! He chose her, and she responded. Mary's first *fiat* is addressed to Joseph. Her second *fiat* is the one she says to the angel, but her first one is to Joseph when she says "yes" to this orientation of her life. Of course, hidden within her heart is a more deeply-rooted orientation, namely, her consecration to God, but this is not an official one; her life is entirely given to God, but in secret. From the public, official perspective, Mary's first orientation is towards Joseph through the *fiat* she said to him and that must have caused a wonderful blossoming in Joseph's heart. It must have been a very great moment for the heart of this just and upright, "God-fearing," God-loving man[101] when he first met Mary and discovered her as the little creature that God had placed upon his path. And Joseph's choice was that: discovering this little creature of such simplicity, so hidden away—"Your eyes are doves behind your veil"[102]—and receiving the smile that revealed her "yes." There was a "knot" here that tied together Joseph's life. It was the Holy Spirit Himself Who was the "knot"[103] that bound together their hearts, their souls and their sensibilities in an extraordinary poverty. This is where we touch upon the greatness and the nobility of love, in fact: love is only noble when it is poor. When love does not have that poverty, it loses its nobility because it becomes possessive, and then the gift is no longer what it should be.

When Mary accepted this choice and responded to it, she inevitably confided her great secret to Joseph—the secret of her consecration to God. She could not have done otherwise; she was obliged to do so in order to be truthful, since she was totally consecrated to God,[104] and if she had not confided it to him there would have been a sort of lie between them. She had made her consecration "if such was God's gracious will,"[105] with the sole desire of fully accomplishing His will, but her gift to God was of such depth that she could not not speak to Joseph about it. Hence we can understand, theologically, the poverty of Joseph's choice and of the choice made by Mary: Mary makes her choice as someone who no longer belongs to herself, and it is because of this that her choice is entirely surrendered to the Holy Spirit. A choice made in total surrender to the Holy Spirit is one that is profoundly poor; one is stripped of everything. When we choose a friend humanly there is always a little possessiveness involved, and Providence takes care of gradually dispelling that aspect… but it takes time and there are tears and hurts. It is entirely different for Mary: in her case there was immediately a clarity of vision and a poverty of spirit. Since she belonged to God alone, she chose Joseph in an initiative of love that was far above the ordinary; for when we belong to God we have a capacity to love that goes much further than when we love humanly. It was God Who, through Mary's heart, loved Joseph and chose him.

In order to receive Mary's love, in order to receive her who was totally consecrated to God, Joseph must have had to enter into this consecration himself. Could we not say, then, that, in choosing Mary, Joseph consecrated himself to God? When Mary told him about herself, Joseph received her as she was, and, since he loved her, his only desire could have been to live what she lived. When we love someone, we receive what is most secret in that person and we desire to live it too. If it were any other way it would be the proof that we do not really love that person, since love is concerned with what is best, most intimate and most secret in a person. Truly choosing to love someone means loving what is most profound in that person. What was deepest in Mary was that she belonged to God. Joseph therefore chose this out of love for her, and so consecrated himself to God by the very fact that he loved her. We could say, in a certain sense, that this is Mary's first act of mediation. Joseph, by loving Mary and choosing her, gives himself totally to God. He was not perhaps fully aware of it at the time, but this was what the Holy Spirit was asking of him and he responded without knowing exactly where this total consecration would lead him. Being given to Mary, he was, by the same fact, completely given to God. This is the loving mediation that Mary's heart performs for Joseph.

The Mystery of the Annunciation

God lost no time in purifying Joseph's heart even further. Unknown to Joseph, the angel had visited Mary alone in Nazareth and Mary had given him her response, also alone. She had replied with a *fiat* of love in which she accepted a gift that infinitely surpassed her. We cannot say the same for the gift that Joseph made to her of his heart; it did not infinitely surpass her. Of course, in her humility, Mary considered Joseph as coming before her and as having an authority to exercise, but we could not say that he loved Mary more than Mary loved him. Indeed, we must say the opposite; Joseph does not transcend Mary. He loved her, and Mary loved him with great poverty and humility, putting him before herself. However, at the Annunciation, the choice that Mary makes in her *fiat* is something altogether different, because it is a choice of the gift that the Father gives her of His Son. This is a gift that completely surpasses her, and it is only in a wholly pure and contemplative faith that she is able to receive it. It is for this reason that this gift plunges her into silence, a silence which binds her to the will of the Father, to the Holy Spirit Who "came upon her"[106] and to the One Who is given to her: her Son. It is impossible for her to communicate this secret.

So Mary keeps the secret of the Annunciation, and she can do so because she trusts Joseph. We share a secret with someone because we trust that person, but sometimes we need to keep silent, and it is the mark of an even greater trust. Mary could ask anything of Joseph, and she asked him to endure this silence. She shared her first secret with Joseph but not her second. This is where we see the difference between the consecration she makes of herself to God and the gift that God gives her, the gift of His Son. This gift takes hold of Mary, possesses her, and thus her *fiat* leads her along a new path of silence.

The Annunciation was such a great event that, at the time, Mary did not reflect upon the difficult situation in which she now found herself, from the point of view of human prudence. Contemplation takes us beyond prudence, and sometimes, because of the demands of contemplation, God places us in situations which are extremely difficult from the point of view of human prudence; Mary had to accept this. She was able to endure it thanks to the presence of Jesus—a presence which was very powerful—and also thanks to her act of fraternal charity towards Elizabeth.

But how is Joseph going to be able to live it? Can God break the unions He makes? God had brought about this extraordinary union between Joseph and Mary, and now He seemed to be breaking it. If we look at it in an exterior way, it would seem that God made every effort to put an end to their union: He wanted Mary to be alone when the angel Gabriel came to visit her, and He wanted her to agree to the message of the angel (that she was to be the Mother of the Son of the Most High) without asking Joseph's consent. Humanly speaking, therefore, there was a breach in her relationship with Joseph. When one is deeply united to someone, one does not make a decisive choice about one's life without asking the advice of the person one loves. In friendship, friends have "the same will" (*idem velle*),[107] and through this they are bound to one another. Now, it would seem, according to the passage in Scripture, that God in fact asked Mary to make her decision at a time when she was alone. "The angel came to her... and the angel left her":[108] only Mary is mentioned. This is understandable from a supernatural standpoint: it is necessary for Mary to make her decision alone. However, we may ask ourselves why it was necessary. Would it not have been simpler if the angel had visited Mary when Joseph was there? Of course, as Matthew tells us,[109] they had not yet come to live together, but Joseph must still have come to visit Mary—maybe to pray the Psalms with her and to worship God with her. The angel could have come at such a time, and God could have allowed Joseph to witness the Annunciation. Even if he had not heard the words of the angel, could he not have been there, at Mary's side? This was, after all, something that was very important for her... But no: the angel came when Mary was alone. Why, then, was it so, if God had united them in such a profound way? Man must not separate what God has joined together.[110] Is God going to separate Joseph from Mary—Mary whom He keeps as the apple of His eye?[111] For we can indeed be sure that God has never kept such a careful watch over any human being as he did over Mary, for His prevenient mercy[112] enveloped her in a unique way. Furthermore, her meeting with Joseph is not without significance for Mary; it was a decisive moment in her life. It is certainly something difficult for her, since she had consecrated herself to God, but it is nevertheless a decisive moment.

Why, then, does God send His angel to Mary when she is alone? It is so that we understand that Mary's covenant with her God is a personal covenant and is greater than any human friendship.[113] She is consecrated to God, and through her motherhood she will be consecrated in a new way, in a way that is yet more profound and more divine. There is, as it were, a double consecration: *elegit eam et praeelegit eam*, as the Latin liturgy used to say for the Office of Virgins: "He chose her and preferred her...." He chose her twice: in the mystery of her virginal consecration and in the mystery of her maternal consecration. This latter consecration was also a personal choice. Mary's *fiat* has to be uttered while she is alone in contemplation; she could only have pronounced her *fiat* in a state of adoration and contemplation, alone before God. She could not have pronounced it jointly with Joseph, because this is not a joint work that she shares with him. It is the personal *fiat* of the virgin consecrated to God who agrees to become the Mother of God, and as such it is something much greater. Those who claim that Joseph was present (which is not Scriptural) are forgetting what exactly a theological relationship to God is. Every theological relationship to God takes hold of us in what is most personal and individual to us. There is nothing more personal than faith and hope, and even more so charity. We can of course proclaim our faith together as a community, but it is firstly something personal. The interior act of faith (and the divine motherhood of Mary is firstly a motherhood in faith, a motherhood of faith) is a personal act that Mary accomplishes by uttering her *fiat*. It is for this reason that she needs to be alone—just as in the beatific vision.[114]

Joseph's New Choice: Mary Expecting the Child Jesus

While Mary was with Elizabeth, Joseph was living with the hope that she would soon return, and his hope in Mary's promise was very strong. He had accepted the separation in a spirit of fraternal charity because Mary had asked it of him, but it was a difficult trial for him to endure. And lo and behold, Mary returns, bearing her treasure... At that moment Joseph must have experienced an even greater trial in the depths of his heart. He could not have doubted Mary's faithfulness[115] (as the Church Fathers understood very well).[116] This passage of Scripture is certainly not very easy to understand, but this is because it hides a secret, and it hides Joseph as well. Joseph is a man who is reserved for Mary alone. The total gift of himself that he makes to Mary hides him, and it is his holiness; it is in being wholly given to Mary that he glorifies the Father.

To come back to the text in Matthew, it is clear that it is not very easy to understand. Yet if we read it carefully, do we not find an indication in the fact that the prophecy of Isaiah is mentioned immediately afterwards? Joseph surely had a good grasp of the Scriptures, given the nobility of his intelligence and heart, and the greatness of his faith, hope and love. Moreover, he was led by the Holy Spirit Himself (one must be close to the Holy Spirit to receive angelic visitations during the night!) Since he was so close to the Holy Spirit and had such a good grasp of Scripture, surely he must have understood that the prophecy of Isaiah about the virgin bearing a child was being accomplished in Mary?[117] And in his poverty and humility, he must have understood that, since this mystery was being accomplished without him, he ought to step aside. Is such "stepping aside" not the great law of love?[118] Faced with someone under the direct influence of the Spirit of God, the only thing for him to do is to disappear and send her back to her own home and to her parents. Not having been warned by God, is that not what he ought to do? He had made a mistake, he had gone too far too quickly; he ought not to have betrothed Mary. Perhaps Joseph blames himself, but he does not blame Mary at all. He was usually such a prudent man, but now he had been imprudent! Sometimes we see that happen—wonderful young men who think themselves unworthy to marry a girl whom they think is too good for them. Joseph must have felt something like that very deeply. She whom he had chosen, she whom he had loved so heroically, in receiving her secret and accepting it, here she was slipping away from him— or at least he thinks so, for he considers himself as being unworthy. In his prudence he believes that the only people who could be the guardians of Mary's secret are her parents; they are such holy people! Joseph believes he would not have the necessary prudence to be the guardian of her whom God has chosen. Being a worker, he does not have the refinement needed, so the only thing to do is to step aside! There is something very great indeed about Joseph's "kenosis" ... It is hard for him, having had the happiness of knowing Mary, to see that he should quietly step back, understanding that this is the right thing to do: God has all the rights over Mary.[119] This is what the "just" man does: he recognizes that God has all the rights. When Mary told him her secret, he ought to have understood that she belonged totally to God, and he should have stepped aside.

This trial plunges Joseph's heart into a suffering from which the "angel of the Lord"[120] comes to rescue him, bringing him an immense and wholly new joy, even greater than the first joy of their betrothal. At the very moment when he understands that he has to leave Mary totally to God, commending her into the hands of the Father by stepping aside, the Father chooses him—Joseph.

But can we stop there? To do so would be to forget that, although the mystery of the Cross has not yet been revealed to him (and he will not live the event of the Cross), Joseph already lives by Christian grace. Therefore he can already understand that beyond human sadness lies a joy which comes from God[121] and which can coexist with what makes us suffer humanly, because divine love makes use of suffering in order to communicate itself even further.[122] Thus we may very well consider that, during the night, before the angel appears to him in a dream, Joseph, plunged like Abraham into the dark night of faith and "hoping against all hope," believes, and thus "becomes a father."[123] He is suffering deeply, but he is not sad with a human sadness (which always entails a turning-in on oneself), because, in him, hope and love are victorious over suffering.

This divine purification of the love of friendship which united the hearts of Joseph and Mary is surely one of the first fruits of the Incarnation.

The first fruit of the Incarnation is for Mary, as it should be. This fruit is the radical purification of her heart, or, to be more precise, the fact that, thanks to a prevenient act of mercy, she had been completely preserved from the stain of original sin.[124] Saint Thomas did not touch upon the mystery of the Immaculate Conception in his *Summa Theologica*, because the Church had not yet made a pronouncement on it. Fr. Mandonnet, a Dominican and a good historian (whom we could not suspect of having mystical intuitions), and who had a thorough knowledge of what Saint Thomas says in the *Summa*, used to say that, given Saint Thomas's love for Mary, he must surely have preached on the mystery of the Immaculate Conception in his sermons! It's quite possible. In the *Summa*, however, Saint Thomas demonstrates that although Mary never had the stain of original sin on her soul, thanks to a prevenient act of mercy, she nevertheless knew the consequences of it in her human nature up until the time of the

Annunciation, and that it was only at the moment of her *fiat* that she became immaculate in terms of the consequences of sin.[125] Saint Thomas saw in this the first effect of the Incarnation in Mary, and that is a beautiful intuition. Thus the first effect of the Incarnation would have been for Mary in the form of a radical purification of her soul in respect to all the consequences of original sin. Is there not a basic intuition in this that we can keep hold of, whilst at the same time correcting it and going further? Mary was immaculate from the moment of her conception, as the Church teaches us. But at the moment of the Incarnation, when she uttered her *fiat* and the Word "became flesh" within her, there was surely a fruit of this presence of the Incarnate Word within her, as a personal gift for her. Wouldn't this gift have been that Mary—bearing the source of all graces, the source of Christian grace—was able to work in cooperation with this source?

In fact, we can see that this is what happens, first with regard to Elizabeth and John the Baptist, then with regard to Joseph. We are in the presence here of a love of friendship, the love of a husband and wife, that is radically purified in a total spiritual poverty, so that the love of the Father might be lived fully in them and in a more perfect way than if Mary and Joseph had been living separately, along side each other. Their love of friendship allows them to be led more easily by the Holy Spirit. It is a journey towards a greater holiness for them, because it allows divine love to become incarnate within their sensibilities, respecting the total gift of self that each one makes to God in a spirit of virginity, in a complete receptivity to the Holy Spirit and in a spirit of poverty (which is what enables them to be receptive to the Holy Spirit). What we see here is a first community which is the last community of the Old Testament, and which prepares the way perfectly for Christian grace. When Joseph receives the order from the angel—his mission to play the role of husband and father—he understands that the covenant between them as husband and wife is not broken; instead it takes on a new dimension through Mary's divine motherhood. And this new dimension is that Mary can ask the Child Jesus, Whom she is carrying within her, to shine forth upon Joseph.

Mary experienced this in the mystery of the Visitation: her act of fraternal charity towards Elizabeth is used by the Holy Spirit to sanctify the tiny John the Baptist, through the presence of the Child Jesus in Mary's womb. Elizabeth herself received the grace of this sanctification and was consequently enlightened about Mary: "Blessed are you among women, and blessed is the fruit of your womb! And why is this granted me, that the mother of my Lord should come to me? ...blessed is she who believed that there would be a fulfillment of what was spoken to her from the Lord!"[126] Mary experienced this presence of the Child Jesus within her in a divine way—this presence capable of purifying and sanctifying the little John the Baptist and his mother. When Mary had returned to Joseph—"Joseph did as the angel commanded him. He took Mary to be his wife"—there surely must have been something mysterious then which bound together the hearts of Joseph and Mary even more profoundly, something which bound them together in a friendship that was all the more free and strong, through and in the presence of Jesus? What the Holy Spirit had done for Elizabeth, He surely does also for Joseph, in a way that is entirely personal to him. Joseph knows that Mary is the mother of God—he knows it from the angel—but when he meets Mary and takes her "into his home," he will "know" it in a much more intimate and profound way—in a way that is very personal and individual. Scripture tells us nothing about this new encounter of theirs, but isn't it up to us to seek to understand it?

"Do not be afraid to take Mary your wife into your home ...":[127] "your wife"—she is doubly his wife since she is chosen once by Joseph and once again by God when events seemed to have annulled their splendid plans. We can recognize in this an echo of Abraham's trial as regards his son Isaac: God asks Abraham to offer up the work that he had accomplished up to that moment. God also asks Joseph to offer up the work that he had accomplished up to then, and to offer it up very radically, not grinding his teeth or grumbling, but going right to the very end in his love for Mary and for his God. This is a very great facet of Joseph's holiness.

As a consequence of this new love he has for Mary, another new love is born in Joseph's heart: his love for the Child Jesus, the true son of her who is his wife. Mary loves this Child Who is given to her by the Father, and everything that belongs to Mary belongs to Joseph, in the light of her consecration to God ("if such be the gracious will of God"). The Father receives Joseph's act of abandon, of total submission, and He wants him to cooperate in his own way in the work being accomplished in Mary through the Holy Spirit.

Every time we put everything into God's hands in this simple and absolute way, God always responds in an infinitely greater way, and His response comes to confirm and renew all that we give Him, by taking it infinitely further. We must ask Saint Joseph to help us to live this secret in our lives.

The Decree from Caesar and the Arrival in Bethlehem

Another trial awaits Joseph: the decree from Caesar.[128] Couldn't God, Who, in His Wisdom and Providence, knows everything, and Who had sent the angel to Mary, have arranged that the decree from Caesar take place either before or after this critical time? No, God knew what He was doing when He allowed the decree from Caesar to be promulgated at the time that Mary was expecting the birth of her son. In his prudence enlightened by the Holy Spirit, Joseph recognizes that he must set off with Mary to Bethlehem, the city of David. She too is undoubtedly of

David's line,[129] but in any case she would have gone with Joseph as his wife, and also as an expectant mother.

Nothing is related about the journey from Nazareth to Bethlehem. We can understand without too much trouble how weary Mary must have been, and how Joseph must have assisted her. But God undoubtedly allows this journey so that the intimacy between Joseph and Mary can grow deeper. It is sometimes during journeys like this which are unplanned or during times of difficulty that people can be drawn closer together, and in this case Joseph is able to help Mary and show her all his tenderness. How he must have longed to be even just once in a situation where he could help Mary! Providence allows him to do just that during this time of waiting. He would not have been able to help her in the same way if they had remained in Nazareth; hence this decree from Caesar is in some way for him. And it is for Mary as well, even more so—so that she can await the arrival of the child Jesus in a greater solitude, and so that she can have a greater intimacy with the tiny child Whom she is carrying. In Nazareth she would have been surrounded by her mother and her immediate family; thanks to Caesar's decree they are able to travel far away and be on their own.

When they arrive in Bethlehem, no one pays any attention to the young mother who is soon to give birth. David's descendants are lacking in courtesy, to say the least (not to mention charity): no room for them at the inn, no room for them in the public house, they are forced to move on. This is something very difficult and humiliating for Joseph. He cannot have accepted very easily such a departure from Bethlehem! It is very hard for him because he is responsible for Mary and for the child Who is to be born; the child is Mary's son, but he too is responsible for Him. His is a double responsibility: he is responsible for the child, because God had designated him for that purpose, and he is responsible for Mary, as her spouse. Joseph, being a just and prudent man, takes this double responsibility to heart. So he leaves the city to find a shelter where they can spend the night and await the hour of the birth of the Son of God.

It was necessary that this Christmas take place in solitude so that Joseph be the sole guardian of the secret of Mary, the Virgin mother. It was necessary that Mary be alone to receive her son, in poverty, so that she might show Him all her love. The first Christmas, for Joseph, Mary and the Child Jesus, was a mystery of extraordinarily strong and tender presence. Before bringing the shepherds in to see Mary, and later the Wise Men, Joseph experiences a new intimacy with her. During those first moments in the presence of the Child Jesus, Mary is full of attention towards her Child, and Joseph weds himself to this attention and enters fully into it. This is where we discover Joseph the contemplative being schooled by Mary in the presence of the Child Jesus. Not only is he careful not to disturb Mary's own contemplation and to be the guardian of the silence and intimacy there, but he lives it himself—not as a spectator but as a witness (a witness being someone who *lives* the mystery he witnesses).

The Prophecy of Simeon and its Fulfillment

Joseph then goes up to the Temple with Mary for the presentation of the child Jesus and for Mary's purification. He is present there and hears the old man Simeon exult with joy when he realizes that he can now depart:

> Lord, now lettest Thou Thy servant depart in peace, according to Thy word; for mine eyes have seen Thy salvation which Thou hast prepared in the presence of all peoples, a light for revelation to the Gentiles, and for glory to Thy people Israel.[130]

Such a confirmation is as wonderful for Joseph as it is for Mary! But immediately afterwards, having giving them both his blessing, the elderly Simeon turns to Mary and says, "Behold, this child is set for the fall and rising of many in Israel, and for a sign that is spoken against and a sword will pierce through your soul also, that the thoughts of many hearts may be revealed." The sword that strikes Mary's heart strikes Joseph's heart too; his heart is wounded, prophetically. We tend to forget this too easily; we consider Joseph's strength and his tenderness, but we must not forget that he received this painful prophecy.

Let us try to penetrate this mystery a little further. If a sword is to pierce Mary's soul, then it is also to pierce Joseph's soul; if not, he would not be her friend. Friends want to bear the same suffering, the same pain, the same burdens—each bearing them in his or her own way. This prophecy is clearly first for Mary, but it is impossible that Joseph could have had a "holy indifference" towards it: "This concerns you; it's something for you. I saw clearly that Simeon was looking at you and not at me..." That would have been completely false! Simeon's prophecy concerns the child Jesus, of Whom Joseph is the guardian. Everything that concerns the child Jesus thus concerns Joseph, and everything that wounds the heart of the wife wounds the heart of the husband. Joseph now understood more fully that he truly was Mary's spouse (as the angel had told him) and the father of the One Who was born of her—Jesus. He could not have not known any more than Mary what was meant by this wounding by the sword, but, like her, he was not afraid of it either. Without knowing, of course, all that the fulfillment of this prophecy would in fact entail, he understood that, if this sword existed, it existed to further their love and to make it more divine (because there is a constant temptation to stop at a practice of love which is merely human and which comes to us more naturally).[131]

Concerning this fourth "joyful" mystery, Saint John Eudes says that this prophecy, which first concerns the Child Jesus—"Behold, this child is set for the fall and rising of many in Israel ..."—is brought to completion in the heart of Mary—"a sword will pierce through your own soul also ... "—and that, since this is so, all the prophecies of the Old Testament about the Messiah find their completion in Mary's heart. This is a very beautiful principle of mystical exegesis as regards Mary. Could we not also add that the prophecy concerning Mary is completed mystically in the heart of Joseph? How could it have been otherwise, since God had united them as husband and wife? Could we not say, then, that all the prophecies of the Old Testament that concern the heart of Mary help us to understand Saint Joseph's heart?

The first fulfillment of this painful prophecy will take place after the visit of the Wise Men, when Joseph will have to take the child Jesus to Egypt because His life is being sought. The second fulfillment will be when Jesus, at the age of twelve, goes up to Jerusalem for the feast of Passover with His parents. Spending this Passover with the twelve-year-old Jesus was certainly an immense joy for Joseph. But when Joseph and Mary leave Jerusalem, the boy Jesus stays behind in the Temple without saying a word to them. This is something inexplicable for Joseph—for Mary also but perhaps even more so for Joseph, because of the authority that he had received from God: had he failed in his duty, in his responsibility? Ought he to have been more careful? These are his thoughts at this moment. Yet he had done all that he ought to have done ... Surely Jesus could have let them know? It would have been so simple! Mary would have agreed; Joseph would have agreed. But no, it was necessary that the hearts of Mary and Joseph know this great suffering; it was necessary that they each cooperate in their own way in this first apostolic work of Jesus among the theologians. Teaching theologians is difficult! Jesus had to set about it at the age of twelve so that He might give the humblest, poorest and meekest lesson possible: a lesson by questioning.

This first "sermon" of Jesus is quite astonishing—a twelve-year-old child questioning the doctors of the Law to compel them to go further and to wake them up to something they had either forgotten or of which they were unaware. Jesus wants to prepare them (it's a long-term preparation, but a merciful one) to receive what He has "heard from His Father."[132] And for this, Joseph had to suffer with Mary, so as to cooperate, in his own way, with Jesus' first apostolic work. Accepting not to understand anything and offering up his deepest desires, he once again "hopes against all hope," like Abraham. This is the first fulfillment of the mystery of the Compassion;[132b] Joseph lives it with Mary. Through Jesus' incomprehensible absence he anticipates, in a certain way, the mystery of the Cross; he is united to this mystery and he draws life from it.[133]

The Hidden Life

We might also look at Joseph's hidden life in Nazareth—the time from their return from Egypt until the moment when God decides that it is time for Joseph to leave this earth. We know nothing about this hidden life, and yet in a way we know everything, if we say that it is a life "hidden with Christ in God."[134] It is a life of prayer, of contemplation, of work (there is no idling; the work is done well, and properly). It is also a life of fraternal charity, that extraordinary fraternal charity which must have existed between Mary and Joseph, as well as between each of them and Jesus.

These intimate years in Nazareth constitute the framework of Joseph's life. It is here that we discover his virtues—virtues which are well hidden but very great indeed. Joseph is without doubt a contemplative.[135] He is also a silent man, both because he is a worker and a contemplative, and also because he loves with an intense love (true silence comes from love). One cannot love Mary with an intense love without entering into her silence, and the presence of the child Jesus, close to Joseph as he works, leads him to an even deeper and more intimate silence. Joseph is a man of silence who combines in a wonderful way contemplation, work, fraternal charity and service. He is a faithful servant, a gentle servant, a poor servant;[136] he gives himself entirely to the service he performs—performed with such great love because he performs it for Mary and for the child Jesus. He exercises authority,[137] but he knows that, because of the Father's love for her and Jesus' love for her, Mary is to teach him to live an ever more profound divine life. He recognizes in Mary someone who is closer to God than he, and this is his great joy. When we love someone deeply we are pleased to be taught by him or her; Joseph was pleased to be taught by Mary, and also by the child Jesus, of course, and yet Joseph was responsible for this Holy Family.

How simple Saint Joseph's holiness is! How close it is to the hearts of men and yet how great, being a hidden holiness and one achieved in silence, in the total gift of himself, wholly given to Mary as her spouse, accepting, from her and from God, this poverty in his heart as a husband—a poverty so as to love even more, but a poverty all the same, imposed by God's Wisdom. It is hard for a man to accept, but if he knows how to go beyond poverty so as to love even more, then it is something very noble. Joseph is the husband *par excellence* and the father *par excellence*—the father of Jesus in an extraordinary poverty, having no claim on his son but giving himself up entirely to Him, because He is the Beloved Son Whom the Father has entrusted to his care.

In this total gift of himself to the child Jesus, Joseph is indeed the "guardian"—*Redemptoris custos*, "called to watch over the Redeemer"—as he is the guardian of Mary's virginity, hiding her not only from the eyes of men but even from the devil, as the Church Fathers said. Saint Ignatius of Antioch wrote: "Mary's virginity and her giving birth escaped the notice of the prince of this world, as did the Lord's death—those three secrets crying to be told, but wrought in God's silence."[138] Citing this passage, Origen adds: "'Mary's virginity escaped the notice of the ruler of this age.' It escaped his notice because of Joseph, and because of their wedding, and because Mary was thought to have a husband. If she had not been betrothed or had not had a husband (as people thought), her virginity could never have been concealed from the 'ruler of this age.'"[139] And Saint Ambrose says: "And there is no ordinary reason why Mary's Virginity deceived the prince of this world, who, when he saw her espoused to a man, could not hold her Birthgiving as suspicious."[140] Joseph thus hides the divinity of Jesus, Whom everyone thinks is "the carpenter's son." It would seem, therefore, that we can say that Joseph prevented the devil from infiltrating the Holy Family during the hidden life. It is to the desert that Jesus will be "led by the Spirit to be tempted by the devil";[141] he cannot attack Jesus in the house in Nazareth: "Upon your walls, O Jerusalem, I have set watchmen…"[142]

3

THE SERVICE OF AUTHORITY

In an age such as the one in which we live, when so much disorder arises from the confusion between authority and power, Saint Joseph is constantly there to remind Christians that authority is a service that God entrusts to someone. Saint Joseph, more than anyone else, exercised his authority as a poor, faithful and meek servant. "Noble Son of David," "Splendor of Patriarchs," as we read in the litanies,[143] Joseph was also a servant, and "the servant is not greater than his master"[144] Who "emptied Himself, taking the form of a slave."[145]

In Saint Joseph there is indeed a mystery of authority, of an authority within a fatherhood that is wholly divine. As Saint Paul says, all fatherhood comes from the Father;[146] with Saint Joseph, the fatherhood of the Father is given to us in a way that is very poor, but at the same time very absolute. This is one of the most important aspects of the mystery of Joseph. His tie with Mary is of course even more important, and is the foundation of this mystery. However, Joseph still remains a man of authority, and in this sense he is truly the one who brings to completion the line of patriarchs.

Paternal Authority

The first three patriarchs, Abraham, Isaac and Jacob, represent the first Covenant, which is a covenant made with fathers. This is understandable, since it is the Father Who is the source of all love within the Most Holy Trinity. But, since nothing is perfect in the first Covenant, this threefold covenant with the fathers is complemented by the covenant with Moses. It is a covenant which remains rooted in the fathers, but Moses is the lawgiver. The people of Israel will eventually claim a third form of covenant, one with the kings. Mankind has a lot of trouble understanding paternal authority, and it's one of the clearest attacks of the devil in the world today: he absolutely cannot stand paternal authority, hence he wants to destroy it, and in order to do so he wants to kill the paternal heart in man. We are aware of the important place that "patricide" holds in Freudian psychoanalysis… and once the father has been killed off then the mother is killed as well, because it's only the father who can protect the mother: she can no longer be a mother if she is not protected by the father.

God had wanted fatherhood to be the sole authority for His people. But the people of Israel let themselves be seduced by Pharaoh and by Egypt (the country which symbolically represents well-being and efficiency). So Israel needed to be brought back to its true vocation by means of the Law: "You shall have no other gods before Me…. You shall not bow down to them or serve them."[147] "You shall love the Lord your God with all your heart, and with all your soul and with all your might."[148] "You shall love your neighbor as yourself."[149] The people of Israel, because of their hardness of heart, forgot that the love which unites the sons to the Father should suffice. So God, Who never grows weary,[150] "sent Moses to them, as ruler and deliverer,"[151] to give them a Law from Him, a law in which the first requirement is adoration.

Moses represents an authority that is very different from paternal authority. His is an authority that is much more visible, so visible, indeed, that after a while the people of Israel will no longer see beyond the authority of the Law. And herein lies the drama. If Israel had been more faithful to the paternal authority of Abraham, of Isaac and of Jacob, if the Law had been more relativized and not seen as an absolute, the Jews would have been able to receive the "shoot of David," the descendant of Abraham; they would have been able to recognize Jesus as the Messiah. It was the Law, taken as an absolute, which prevented them from doing so.

Moses, "the servant of the Lord,"[152] who "found favor in [His] sight,"[153] is someone very great indeed; it was his disciples who became intolerable. Moses is a brilliant man whom God raised up to restore to His people the sense of their vocation through adoration. It is, in fact, through adoration that the people of Israel should have rediscovered the meaning of their vocation, and hence paternal authority, because it is only adoration that can give us the sense of the authority of God the Father, source of all life and all love. This paternal authority is obviously above the Law; it may, of course, give individual commandments, but properly and formally it is not at the origin of the Law. It is more than the Law; it is a living law, because it is Love. Yet, because of their infidelity, the people of Israel need a written law, a juridical authority, which God gives to them through the intermediary of a lawgiver.

And in their desire for glory, the people of Israel finally demanded a king,[154] a royal authority, although God would have preferred that their sole authority be a paternal one.

This overview of the history of Israel, with the distinction between the three successive authorities—paternal, legal and royal—ought to help us to understand the role of Joseph in the Church. God radically renews everything in the New Covenant, and He does so from within a family. The Divine Economy is tied to the family. We might think that such a renewal should have taken place out in the desert... In the midst of our daily lives, with so many things to do, we sometimes begin to dream of the desert; it has a seductive power over us: "If I were really alone, then I could worship God, then I could really live this covenant of love in my life...." But no: God wants to renew everything from within a family.

Furthermore, what is so remarkable about the Holy Family is that everything begins anew with the Woman. The New Covenant is made in Mary's heart, whereas the first Covenant had been made in the heart of Abraham. Abraham is a father in his faith that justified him.[155] His fatherhood was indeed "divine," and doubly so (first because of his own faith, and also because of our faith: he is "the father of believers"),[156] yet his fatherhood according to flesh and blood, whilst miraculous, was not in itself "divine." The fruit of this fatherhood is the "son of the promise," but not the Son of God. The New Covenant has a much more profound requirement: it will culminate in the very mystery of the Son of God. This is why it is accomplished in a motherhood that is virginal and divine: to show that it goes beyond flesh and blood. Yet what goes beyond flesh and blood does not go against flesh and blood. The New Covenant is brought about in an incarnation. When God renews everything, He does not eliminate or cancel out anything He has done previously. Mary is to live a divine motherhood both in faith and according to the flesh.

The Holy Family thus represents a radical renewal of everything, a renewal carried out in Mary's heart; Mary is the guardian of paternal authority, and, with her, paternal authority rediscovers its strength. There is a new order. We need to be very attentive to the fact that, in the Old and New Covenants, we find the same elements but in a different order. The order of the Holy Spirit is an order of love, and not an order according to Cartesian logic. The "logic" of the Holy Spirit is that of love blossoming according to an order of wisdom. Everything is renewed through Mary's heart, and Joseph's paternal authority is itself inscribed in Mary's heart.

There is something completely new here: paternal authority is now linked to the mystery of a source, of a maternal fruitfulness which comes directly from God. In her virginal motherhood Mary is linked directly to the Father; it is in Him that she is "source."

Let us try to understand Joseph's paternal authority. It is far greater than that of the patriarchs, for it is an authority over the Son of God. Authority varies in greatness according to the people over whom it is exercised. Is this not the reason why Scripture tells us that "the Lord honors the father in his children"?[157] Hence we can see what exactly Joseph's authority must have been—an authority which will be glorified by Christ's priesthood, by the Beloved Son of the Father! Joseph holds authority over Him Who is the Beloved Son. Why? Because he is linked to Mary. We see the difference between the relationship between Abraham and Sarah, and between Mary and Joseph... Mary is the Woman— she who is totally relative to God, immaculate, entirely pure, entirely loving. Because she is wholly bound to God, she is more woman than any other woman. She has a heart that is more tender, more loving, more capable of loving, and hence she is more closely bound to Joseph than any other wife could ever be bound to her husband. She is bound to him in a much more profound and stronger way, and Joseph's authority derives from this bond with Mary, and from this intimacy between them that is willed by God. In this sense we could almost say that his authority is "mediated" by Mary; but it is also an authority which directly represents the Father's own. It is therefore an authority which, in a certain sense, is absolute, and this is perhaps the secret of Mary's mediation: she does not relativize anything. We are used to mediators who relativize what they mediate by imposing themselves. Mary's mediation is so unlike any mediation of that sort that she herself could be subject to Joseph's authority at the same time. Joseph's authority comes to him from God through Mary, and Mary is subject to Joseph...

Two Secrets

Joseph is first of all Mary's husband. This is the first thing revealed to us. He is revealed in relation to Mary, and she to him. We do not know how they came to meet, but we know that a meeting took place, and that consequently Mary becomes "betrothed to Joseph"—an encounter so absolute that they love each other and mutually choose each other. Which of them chose the other first? If we adhere to the normal cultural conditions of the people of Israel at that time, then it was Joseph who chose Mary and Mary who responded, confiding to Joseph a prior secret she had—that of her consecration.[158] Joseph's choice must therefore have been the work of the Holy Spirit, and in making it he shows a remarkable audacity. He did not have a very clear understanding of what he was doing, but at the same time he knew that it was an extraordinary grace. Living a life of faith as he did, he could sense who Mary was and sense it very profoundly, since she had revealed to him her total consecration to God. The Church has upheld this truth with the celebration of the feast of Mary's Presentation in the Temple. We know nothing about it historically—we know none of the details[159]—and the ways in which painters have depicted Mary's Presentation in the Temple, admirable though their various ways may be, remain at the level of devotion. But in faith we have to affirm that Mary consecrated herself totally to God, in accordance with His gracious will. Mary shared her secret with Joseph, because otherwise he could not have chosen her in all truth. He needed to know that her whole being was given to God, otherwise there would have been "an error concerning the person," as Canon Law says. Now, there could be no error regarding the person here, because Joseph had only one desire: to do the will of God fully. And when we want to do the will of God fully, and to do only that, then God enlightens us and helps us to understand the truth.

The realism of love requires our going as far as this. Mary is a unique being: just think of the mystery of the Immaculate Conception! This mystery was undoubtedly not revealed explicitly to Joseph, but it was revealed to him that, for God, Mary was unique—that she was God's treasure and that God loved her in such a way that the whole of Creation was renewed in her. When we love we have a great audacity. On learning of Mary's secret, Joseph had the extraordinary audacity to continue, and to say "yes." There was a mutual *fiat*. The important thing to understand is that Joseph, who has no authority yet, freely chooses Mary. And Mary enlightens him. In the humility of her heart, she helps him see that she is the poorest and the very least of all creatures. She does not say, "You don't know what a great treasure you are taking into your home." No, she says, "You don't know my poverty; I no longer belong to myself, so I can only give myself as someone who is poor, someone who, being totally bound to God, no longer belongs to herself..."

This must have been a wonderful moment, which we too can live through our faith—the faith of tiny children who, because they are so small, can ask for everything. We need to penetrate this moment to discover Joseph's heart, to discover what the Holy Spirit put into his heart at that moment, how he saw Mary; for he saw her as God sees her, since it was God Who enabled him to choose Mary truly and to receive the secret that she had totally delivered herself up to God in accordance with His gracious will. Joseph receives the secret of Mary's consecration; he keeps it safe and he takes Mary into his home.

Next there is a second secret: the loving "theft" of Mary by God in the mystery of the Annunciation. This is a secret for Mary, betrothed to Joseph. God sometimes likes to accomplish His masterpieces by means of quite extraordinary human complications. When we look at how the mystery of the Annunciation is brought about, we may well say that the angel ought to have been sent to Mary before she was betrothed to Joseph; that would have been much simpler! But God wanted it to be otherwise. It was necessary that Mary be promised and given to Joseph, and that Joseph had accepted her fully. Joseph himself, through Mary, needed to be totally consecrated to God; he needed to have entered into Mary's poverty, to have agreed to receive this marvelous gift from God, and to offer it to God. Joseph always offers Mary, and he offers her because she is wholly given to him. In this sense he lives the royal priesthood of the faithful in an eminent way.

Why, then, is Joseph not with Mary when the angel brings her the message that she will be the Mother of the "Son of the Most High"? He does not strictly speaking have any "authority" over her, but is he not responsible for her, in love? If Mary must be alone at this moment, it is because this is a secret that could only be communicated within contemplative adoration. In contemplative adoration we are always alone with God. It is for this reason that Joseph could not be present. A secret such as the one communicated by the angel is a secret that is one of contemplative life; it is the very secret of the Father—the Word, fruit of His contemplation—which is communicated to Mary. Such a secret can therefore only be communicated within the realism of a wholly contemplative faith, which is itself a participation in God's own life.[160] The bonds of fraternal charity that unite Mary to Joseph are of course very great indeed and very "divine"; they are in a way the ultimate fruit of the Old Covenant, and its culmination. But the radical anticipation, the ultimate disposition to Christian contemplation, at the first moment of the New Covenant in the "Word made flesh," remains adoration and the desire for contemplation.

This point needs to be emphasized, because today we often exalt a false fraternal charity—false because true fraternal charity is rooted in loving adoration, and is the most excellent fruit of that adoration. By degrading charity and reducing it to a human level, we consider only its external aspect, that is, the efficiency in human relationships to which it normally leads. We fall into the realm of the quantitative, and we are no longer able to understand the absoluteness of the solitude of someone who worships with love and who, through his adoration, brings the whole world to God. Thus we then think that Joseph's presence at the Annunciation is necessary because, from the social perspective, he is the authority and the "principal party" in this little community, and therefore (so we think) enables Mary to be more open to the Holy Spirit.

No, from God's perspective Mary is first. Therefore, by means of His angel (in order to allow her a greater freedom), the Father addresses her in the solitude of her loving and contemplative adoration to ask her if she will agree to be the Mother of the Son of the Most High. And this second secret plunges Mary into silence. But the angel gives her a sign: "And behold, your kinswoman Elizabeth in her old age has also conceived a son..."[161] This is always what God does: when He places us in very difficult situations He asks us for the cooperation of our prudence. He gives Mary a sign not for her faith but for her prudence. Divine prudence requires us to keep God's secrets when He asks us to keep them. This is surely one of the most eminent acts of Christian prudence, and it is one of the most difficult things in the world today, which is a world of propaganda. A lot of journalists are people who dig out other people's secrets; in those situations we need a divine prudence and a lot of shrewdness: "...be wise as serpents and innocent as doves."[162] Divine prudence helps us see that we need to do all we can to keep the secret. Mary understood that this was the case, even with regard to Joseph. Her silence is not a lack of trust on her part. It is because God wants it to be like that; it is a case of God's sovereign rights.

God gives this sign to Mary for Joseph's sake: she is to go to Elizabeth's house and stay there for three months. We should think often about these first three months that Mary spent expecting Jesus, because the fact that they took place at Elizabeth's service is something quite remarkable. God asks Joseph to accept this poverty, and he asks it of Mary also. For it is hard for her not to be with Joseph. Elizabeth is very nice, but, all the same, an elderly cousin is not quite the same as Joseph! He is a support, a comfort and an aid to her; she trusts him so much! But she is deprived of this support in order to remain more deeply in the secret, whilst exercising fraternal charity towards Elizabeth.

The Trial Concerning Authority

It is when Mary comes back to him in Nazareth that Joseph realizes that she is expecting a child. And once again, Mary says nothing: she cannot communicate God's secret. She is bound so closely to contemplation of the Father! And the contemplation of the Father has as its fruit the Word of God... Mary lives the silence of the Most Holy Trinity—a communication of love in silence. Bound to this contemplation of the Father, hidden in the silence of the Most Holy Trinity, Mary not only continues to love Joseph but loves him with an even greater love. The more she is united to God, the more she loves Joseph. But she cannot say anything to him; all she can do is to beg God to enlighten him. Could we not say that it is thanks to Mary's prayer that the angel comes to enlighten Joseph? But it is also thanks to Joseph's own prayer, to his own uprightness and to his desire to accomplish fully the will of God.

And so we come to that very moving moment which we have already considered, but which we now look at from the point of view of authority. For in the situation in which this young man, who is a prudent man, now finds himself—namely, doubting his own judgment and his prudence—we can clearly see a trial concerning authority.[163] Joseph is tested in his authority and in his love for Mary. It is not a temptation, it is a trial, which is something altogether different. It is a trial to purify his heart, so that his heart might become poorer and so that he place his heart directly under the guidance of the Holy Spirit. When we exercise authority, there is a tendency to trust only to one's own prudence (in the noble sense of the word),[164] because he who has authority exercises prudence to the highest degree. Mary leaves Joseph completely free; she says nothing, she remains silent. She loves Joseph, and she "carries" him in her heart, but she says nothing. How Joseph would have liked Mary to say something! But she says nothing; she cannot say anything. So it must be the angel who enlightens Joseph. This represents a purification for Joseph's heart, but it also shows us that God leaves him complete authority. If Mary had told Joseph what he ought to do, Joseph's authority would have been founded upon what Mary said. But God wants Joseph's authority to be founded directly upon His own. Such is the authority that Joseph is to exercise over Mary.

It is always very difficult to have to exercise authority over someone who is holier than oneself. We think that, since that person is holier, he or she must receive special graces and lights which I do not receive. But no, God does not want that; that would no longer be the exercise of authority. Mary, who is holier than Joseph, asks God to enlighten him directly, so that his authority is a divine authority. So it is then that the angel comes to enlighten Joseph. Just as God had sent the angel Gabriel to Mary in order to leave her a greater freedom, in the same way He sends the angel to Joseph so as to allow him a greater freedom. The sending of the angels is to safeguard Mary and Joseph's liberty.[165]

Having been enlightened by God, it is still Joseph himself who has to make the decision to stay with Mary. Here he makes a new choice,[166] and in his response to God's will for him we see the birth of Joseph's authority over the Son of God.

Joseph could have said, "No, this is impossible; I am being placed in a false position." This is what we would reply today, in the name of sincerity: "I can't do it. Everybody will think that I am the father of this child Who is really the Son of God; it's quite impossible." But authority does not depend on sincerity. We should always remember this, because we always tend to judge authority at the level of sincerity, and consequently we no longer understand it. Authority does not depend on sincerity; it depends on the truth of the order of God's wisdom for us.

In his prudence enlightened by faith, Joseph understood this. He understood that he had to perform this heroic act; for it was a heroism of love. He performs it also with joy, of course, and with an immense joy, for there is such a thing as a heroism of joy; painful heroism is not the only sort—there is also sometimes joyful heroism, when we are asked to surpass ourselves in an extreme yet joyful way. Joseph performs a heroic act by taking into his home her whom God had chosen to be the Mother of the Son of the Most High—she in whom the Spirit of God has been at work, she who is inhabited by God, she who is loved in this unique way. Joseph was not jealous of God; he did not think of God as a rival, taking away the one who belonged to him, his betrothed.

When the angel says, "For that which is conceived in her is of the Holy Spirit," he highlights the fact that Mary has obeyed the Holy Spirit, obeyed the will of God, and that, concerning Joseph, her position remains exactly the same. It was not she who chose to be Mother of God: God chose this for her, and she accepted it. The angel therefore allows Joseph to receive Mary and to love her in a new way, but in a way which is nonetheless in continuity with his first love for her. Nothing has been broken (only God could arrange things thus). The first tie between them is intensified; it takes a new direction but does so within a continuity—there is no rupture. "She shall bear a son, and you shall call His name Jesus." With these words (which show such a wonderful delicateness on the part of God) the angel gives Joseph authority over the child. Since this child is to be born "of the Holy Spirit," we might envisage that Joseph will be there for Mary, as the guardian of the Virgin Mother, but that the child Jesus will be entirely and solely under Mary's care. Just because Joseph chose Mary as his wife does not mean that he would, of necessity, have authority over the One Who would be born of her through the direct working of God. It is not taken for granted, and that is why the angel underscores the role that Joseph will have: "You will call His name Jesus." Each of the angel's words carries weight[167] and allows us to understand the role that God is giving to Joseph. Naming a newborn child is something that comes under the authority of the father, and, in performing this task, the father acts as God's instrument. For surely to name a tiny child is already to point him in a certain direction. And this is how Joseph is to name the child: "You shall call His name Jesus, for it is He Who will save His people from their sins."

So Joseph is to take Mary into his home—Mary who is now expecting her child—and must understand that he is to exercise authority over Him Whom she will bring into the world through the working of the Holy Spirit. He is to have a paternal authority over Him, an authority in faith, hope and charity. He is therefore to educate Him and be responsible for Him.

Authority and Poverty

Joseph now enters into a new poverty, and we might say that he represents the alliance between authority and poverty. This is perhaps the essential point that we should try to understand here, namely, that authority in the New Covenant is an authority in poverty. Poverty requires us to let God take first place and not to stop at our own judgment. We are rich when we act according to our own judgment, whereas we are poor when we allow God to take precedence over our own opinions, desires, plans, and aspirations. Think of Saint John the Baptist in the desert: he lets the Lamb go before him.[168] Joseph is also in a certain kind of "desert" for his heart. When he is suffering in anguish, no longer knowing what to do, is it not a terrible desert for Joseph? He loves Mary, but because of what he has discovered he can no longer take her into his home. What should he do? We can easily understand the dismay of this just man who remains faithful to Mary but who is overwhelmed by what is happening. It is a very great poverty for a man to accept a situation that is beyond him. Exercising "divine" authority means accepting to be placed in situations in which events are, in fact, beyond us all the time. This is the authority of someone poor—someone who, instead of seeking to dominate (as we do so easily), exercises his authority as nothing but a service of love, without claiming any rights (and consequently having no power).

Thus Joseph is Mary's husband, whilst having no rights whatsoever as a husband. In the sacrifice he makes of his bond with Mary, when he realizes she is with child, he offers the very hope of his husband's heart.

But it is precisely this poverty that allows him to remain Mary's husband. What could have been lived as a rupture is instead lived as a new bond. Only those who are poor can understand this. There are events which can be interpreted as ruptures or, on the contrary, as divine means which allow us to go further. This is what the mystery of the Annunciation was for Joseph: a means given to him by God to go further. There was a moment when Joseph asked himself if this was the will of God, but we should understand this clearly: it was not a temptation to which he succumbed; he simply asked himself what was God's will for him. He first of all chose poverty and decided to step aside. Then when the angel told him to go beyond his fear—"Do not be afraid to take Mary your wife into your home"—he "did as the angel commanded him," and did so in a true choice: he chooses to take Mary and also to keep her secret, the secret communicated in silence. No doubt Mary smiled at Joseph. She could not tell him the secret herself, but Joseph could talk to her; he could tell her that he had had a dream, a message from the angel which had shaken him during the night, and that now he understood everything. And Joseph is then a source of joy for Mary because he is docile to the will of God. And Joseph receives Mary: he receives her into his home, just as John, later on, will receive Mary into his home.[169]

John the Baptist, Joseph and John: three different relationships with the mystery of Mary, with her silence, with her secret. But the one who has authority is Joseph; he is the one who had authority, in a very deep poverty. He was the guardian of Mary's secret. The greatest task of authority—and it is this that requires the greatest strength—is to keep God's secret, in order to allow God's work to be fully accomplished.

It is at this point that we should try to look at the different stages of Joseph's silence. He guards the secret so that Mary can await her child in peace; he allows Mary's heart to be in peace—authority should always bring peace. And he allows Mary, the young Virgin Mother, to await her Son with joy.

Next, he goes to Bethlehem with Mary. Here his authority shows itself first in the decision he takes to go up to Bethlehem for the census:

> And all went to be enrolled, each to his own city. And Joseph also went up from Galilee, from the city of Nazareth, to Judea, to the city of David, which is called Bethlehem, because he was of the house and lineage of David, to be enrolled with Mary, his betrothed, who was with child.[170]

We see here an act of Joseph's authority, an act which is all the more courageous for the fact that "while they were there, the time came for her to be delivered."[171] Despite this, as the time of the birth draws nearer, Joseph takes the responsibility of taking his spouse to Bethlehem. He respects Caesar's decree—"Render therefore to Caesar the things that are Caesar's and to God the things that are God's."[172] Joseph could very well have considered that, given the special circumstances of this birth, he might be exempt from obeying Caesar's decree ... but these decrees must have been quite compulsory. He takes on this responsibility because he thinks he ought to be obedient, even despite the circumstances which, from a human point of view, would have exempted him from this census. Joseph obeys the decree and Mary obeys Joseph. Joseph has a triple authority here: as son of David, as chosen by God, and as having chosen Mary as his spouse.

Once they arrive in Bethlehem, Joseph suffers deeply in his paternal authority. Rejected by those who, like him, are descendants of David, his only option is to shelter Mary in a stable, in a dwelling set aside for animals, so that she can bring into the world "that Child Whom [the descendants of David], who are unbelieving, think base."[173] In this way God tests Joseph's authority, so that he might exercise it with meekness.

The exercise of his authority is also marked by the utmost discretion. When the Wise Men from the East arrive at "the place where the child was," they enter the house, seeing only Jesus and Mary: "going into the house they saw the child with Mary His Mother, and they fell down and worshipped Him."[174] They do not even see Joseph. This shows us how much he is already a child of Mary,[175] someone who remains hidden each time God does not ask him to show himself.[176] But from the "children," the "little ones," Joseph is not so well hidden: the shepherds do see him.[177] Jesus will later say, "I thank Thee, Father, Lord of heaven and earth, that Thou hast hidden these things from the wise and learned, and revealed them to babes." [178] Isn't this how God looked upon Saint Joseph? He is truly one of these "little ones," and this is what makes him great.

At the Nativity, therefore, Joseph's poverty is no longer only in his heart as a husband but also in his heart as a father. The man of poverty is someone who enables certain things to happen, without playing any part in them himself, without actually "doing" anything. He lets everything happen in his presence as if he were in some sense responsible for it whereas in fact he is not. It is very hard to see something come to fruition without having had a hand in it, when normally we would have helped, and everyone thinks we have been involved! This takes an extremely great poverty. We attach such great importance to having a visible responsibility, a charge, a function, and we find it very hard to be poor in the function that God gives us. Sometimes we have to accept that things which should normally have been done with us are done without us, and are done with the help of someone who apparently has nothing to do with it. In Joseph's case, the person Who acted in his place is the Holy Spirit, which makes it infinite! Would we have kept silent if we had been in Joseph's place? Keeping silent is a great poverty: we all love to tell our own stories.

Joseph remains silent, and there is no bitterness in him. On the contrary, it is a deep joy for him to be the one who will accompany Mary and Jesus, hiding them, and protecting them in the strong sense of the word.

The next decision that Joseph has to make is to leave for Egypt, and afterwards to come back to Nazareth. In each case, God gives Joseph an order, through the intermediary of His angel, and it is in this light that he exercises his authority as father and husband—an authority founded upon his love for Mary, and which has its origin in his total docility to the will of the Father.

Joseph will also experience, in a very purifying way, his total dependence upon the Heavenly Father in the exercise of his authority in the fifth "joyful" mystery[179]—after which Scripture tells us that the child Jesus went down again with them to Nazareth, and "was obedient to them."[180]

But Simeon's prophecy has been fulfilled for the first time. The sword, the "Why?" that pierced Mary's soul, has pierced Joseph's soul as well. The same sword pierces both their souls. This is why Joseph is so great: he too participated in the vocation of Christ the priest—this child Who immolates their hearts as He teaches the doctors of Israel, and Who thereby already unites them to His own offering to the Father on the Cross.

All of this helps us to see that Joseph's vocation is not limited to the Holy Family: that, through the heart of Christ, his vocation is open to the mystery of Redemption, and that Joseph becomes, with Mary, someone who cooperates with the mystery of the Cross.

4

MAN OF PRUDENCE

Perhaps it would be helpful to begin by recalling what prudence is. In current terminology, if someone is described as "prudent" it can have slightly negative connotations: someone is prudent if he does not like to make decisions and never commits himself. We readily say that someone is "too prudent," whereas, in fact, someone is never too prudent, since prudence is a summit—a summit between two contrary aspects of the passions.[181] Prudence makes us lucid; it allows us to grow in our love, whether it be at the human or the Christian level. Prudence is also what enables us to be faithful.

Human Prudence

Prudence is that practical wisdom which allows us to choose the means to our human end. We are only prudent if we have chosen a truly human end, that is to say, not simply a goal, but a good that we love and that is capable of perfecting us. Therefore, ultimately, we can only be prudent if we have discovered the existence of God, the existence of the Creator, and if we try to put an order into everything in the light of this. There can be no prudence if there is no finality.

The two great ends, in the human order, are contemplation and friendship. Prudence consists in becoming aware of our intellectual capacities and of our affective (in the broader sense) capacities—the capacities of our will; it means becoming aware of the capacities that we have acquired and of all our human strengths, so that we can order our lives in the most direct way possible towards the end that we are pursuing. The virtue of prudence is that. It is acquired: we become prudent (and it must be acknowledged that this is the virtue most lacking among young people today).

The virtue of prudence is at the heart of what the ancients called the "cardinal virtues": prudence, justice, fortitude and temperance.[182] These four virtues are interlinked. One cannot perform an act of justice, for example, without performing an act of prudence, nor an act of obedience without also performing an act of prudence. We must always bear this in mind. When Joseph obeys the angel, or obeys Caesar's decree, he does not obey like a robot: he obeys using his prudence. This is why it is completely wrong to claim that virtue puts us in a state of slavery; it's quite the opposite. Whereas being dependent upon realities inferior to us diminishes us, we are ennobled by being dependant upon realities (persons) superior to us. Ever since Nietzsche and Freud, the virtue of obedience has been greatly scorned; we must therefore re-establish it by showing that it in fact gives us a new strength. We discover this in the life of Saint Joseph. When it comes to Jesus, He died in obedience;[183] hence, from the Christian perspective, obedience is something vitally important. Generally speaking, it allows us to cooperate with someone greater than ourselves, and cooperating with someone greater than ourselves enables us to grow and to do something that is otherwise beyond us.

The human person, as such, is founded upon the acquisition of prudence. We cannot be a true human person unless we have acquired a certain prudence. From the human perspective, prudence consists firstly in knowing oneself (Socrates' "Know thyself")—knowing oneself objectively, knowing who we are and what are our capacities. There is nothing more ridiculous than someone not very clever who wants to appear to be more clever than he is; however, someone who has only an average intelligence (and who knows it) can, thanks to the virtue of prudence, make wonderful use of the intelligence he has. We do not have to be a genius to be prudent; we need to be attentive to our habits and to our past failings. When we have been unhappy in a particular circumstance, then we try to find out why; we try to find out in what way we lacked justice, fortitude or temperance. Perhaps we let ourselves get carried away by our passions and our passions took over (the passions linked to the imagination are responsible for most setbacks). In a world in which everything serves to develop the imagination, and by the same token the passions, we end up with the so-called "liberation" of the passions, which in actual fact consists in acting solely according to our passions. When this happens there's no prudence any more; it is completely stifled.

In psychological terms, we would say that prudence consists in "managing" all our energy resources. Someone who is prudent takes action advisedly, at the right moment, and he commits himself fully, going right to the very end, engaging all his passions, so that he can achieve what he intends to do. Prudence thus enables us not to waste time, and it makes us sufficiently attentive to the circumstances that present themselves—be they good or bad—so that we engage ourselves at the right moment. This is what is proper to prudence.

Thus there is a prudence at the human level, which is directed towards love, towards friendship. Our greatest education concerns love of friendship, and this is critically important. We must recognize that in good Christian families people have often been brought up to be very virtuous but have been taught very little about loving. Strictly speaking, of course, you cannot teach someone to love. Why? Because love implies a self-education, that is to say, a knowledge of who we are. In the human order, it is this self-education to do with friendship love that gives meaning to our lives, because love needs to be continually growing. Friendship is always friendship with a human person, and consists in loving someone for that *person's own sake*—so we first need to discover that person. In the beginning we love someone for his eyes, for his gaze, for his elegant manner, for his intelligence... and then, little by little, we love his *person*, and that's when we begin to discover him. Love of friendship—that is, true spiritual love—consists in loving a human person for him or herself, beyond his qualities and abilities. Love requires us to go always further, until we reach the *person* whom we love, and reach him in the sense that he is my *good*. The person I love is my *good*, that is to say, he or she is the person who gives meaning to my whole life. And I can always love him more. Being prudent, from the human point of view, means ordering my whole life in such a way as to allow this human love, this love of friendship, to go ever deeper and further. This is at the heart of all human ethics.[184]

Christian Prudence

The prudence of the Christian "assumes" human prudence, for Christian ethics destroys nothing of that which is human. Everything that is human can become Christian, and everything that is Christian is supremely human. The Church Fathers asserted this, understanding that Christian grace, which is like leaven,[185] does not destroy the human "dough" but purifies it and brings it something greater. Everything that is human is waiting to be assumed by charity, including, therefore, friendship love, which is man's finality. In today's world it is vital to understand what friendship love is, for both a human education and a Christian one, since it is always through friendship that things either become corrupted or are elevated (we are aware of the importance of our encounters with people in our lives).

So the Holy Spirit asks us to acquire prudence. Even though He gives us charity, it does not mean that He will substitute Himself for our prudence. We should not say, "I am a Christian, therefore that makes me prudent." Far from it! We are Christians, and so we do indeed have grace, and the theological virtues of faith, hope and charity given to us as a wonderful gift from God, but we are responsible before God for our growth in faith, hope and charity. We need to understand that our person, at the Christian level, is in our being bound to Christ, in becoming the friend of Christ through being His servant, and in loving our neighbor with the aim that our charity becomes incarnate in a friendship with that person, if possible. And we must also realize that our faith allows us to have a Christian prudence, that is to say that it allows us to direct all our activities as far as possible towards Christ—whilst acknowledging that the moral virtues of justice, prudence, fortitude and temperance still need to be acquired.

To follow Christ in this way is to go with Him to the Father: "And this is eternal life: that they know Thee, the only true God…"[186] Hence Christian prudence, by faith, orientates our whole life towards the beatific vision. When Saint Thomas asks whether faith is necessary, he says that it is necessary for the orientation of one's whole life towards the beatific vision. We are made to see God; the necessity of faith lies here. In other words, Christian grace gives us a new finality, one which is beyond our earthly lives.[187]

Christian prudence assumes the human prudence that we acquire, but it has a perspective that goes much deeper and much further, because our prudence transformed by grace (thus by faith and charity), is at the service of our gaze towards God. We are made for the beatific vision; we need to tell ourselves this often, for hope is just that. Every time that we pray the "Our Father" we should immediately understand that we are made to see God face to face. This is the greatness of Christian grace. We are made to live the life of the Trinity, the very life of God—to live it being dependent upon God, of course, but to live it as God lives it. This is what is so extraordinary, and this is what gives the contemplative life its sense. To choose the contemplative life is to understand that we are made for the beatific vision and hence to want to take the quickest route there.[188]

Christian prudence may be exercised in a merely human way, but it may also be transformed by the gift of counsel, which allows for a "divine" exercise of prudence. What does this mean? It means that the end—that towards which we are striving—becomes much closer to the means, and that all the means are ordered in the light of the end. This is what the gift of counsel does, and it is not something reserved for those in the religious life! The prudence of a Christian, of a father or a mother of a family, is still a prudence which leads to the beatific vision, and therefore directly to prayer, to silent prayer. Silent prayer is something normal for a Christian; a Christian should spend time in silent prayer. We know what Saint Teresa of Ávila says: in times of crisis we must make use of especially strong means; and these especially strong means are interior prayer, silent prayer. In our world today, we are indeed living in a time of crisis. In his encyclical Veritatis Splendor, the Holy Father declared that there was a crisis of truth today, and it's true. This is why all Christians who want to lead a fully Christian life today must set aside time for silent, interior prayer. It is necessary. Admittedly, people who are very committed to their work are overloaded today; it can be very difficult for them to set aside time for silent prayer. But as soon as they can, they must do so. True Christians use their holidays to give more time to prayer, to deepen their Christian life: to know the Gospel better, to know Jesus better, to discover what interior, silent prayer is.

What is silent prayer? In his commentary on the Gospel of John, Saint Thomas tells us that "mystically"—that is, in the light of the Holy Spirit—the wedding feast at Cana shows us the mystery of silent prayer, that is to say, of the union of one's soul with Jesus.[189] Silent prayer is about living the most secret and deepest covenant of one's Christian life: the union of one's soul with Jesus, expressed in the Old Testament by the Song of Songs and which we can discover, in the Gospel of John, throughout the apostolic life of Jesus. Silent prayer transforms one's heart into Christ's heart, and does so thanks to the divine exercise of the virtues of faith, hope and charity, which permit and bring about this transformation of one's heart into Christ's heart—the unity of one's heart with His own heart.

Saint Thomas highlights the fact that Mary is invited to the wedding feast at Cana. Each time that we try to pray in silence (to "do" silent prayer) Mary is invited; she is present, and this is even where she carries out her role as mother in the most perfect way. She teaches us to live our Christian life, that is to say, to discover the presence of Jesus close to us and within us. The Christian life is the discovery of Christ looking at us; it is discovering this love that Christ has for us first—"He loved us first"[190]—and responding to this love. If Jesus were not looking at us, we would not be able to contemplate Him. But because He is looking at us—"Jesus, looked at him and loved him"[191]— we are carried towards Him by charity and drawn to live what He Himself lives in relation to the Father, but in the darkness of faith.[192] Discovering Jesus' gaze upon us is indeed the mystery of silent prayer, the anticipation of the beatific vision; we bring it forward, so to speak. One day we shall see clearly how much Jesus loves us and how much we are carried by Him, enveloped by His love and enveloped by His blood. But what we shall see one day in full light, we see already, here on earth, through the veil of faith; we know that it is so. Mary is thus invited, so as to carry our souls towards Jesus, to help us go more directly to Jesus, without being afraid; we must ask Mary to teach us to love Jesus and the Father.

Joseph's Prudence

Let us now see how Saint Joseph is the model of Christian prudence for us. If he has always been considered as such, it is most likely because on many occasions he found himself in very difficult, very tricky circumstances, and had to discern carefully the end and the means to use to attain it. We should examine (and this would be very interesting for a theology of Saint Joseph) all those moments when he had to make a choice, because it is in the choice that prudence is properly formed—the choice of a particular means with a view to an end, with a view to what we need to achieve, with a view to being faithful to the will of the Father.

The first choice that Joseph makes is his choice concerning the person of Mary. Joseph chose Mary, and this is something admirable, even if, in those times, the choice that a man made of a wife was not exactly the same as it is for us today.[193] Families played a determining role here, because marriage was not considered to be simply a personal act; it was also an act that concerned the family. Nowadays we have a terribly individualistic conception of the person, and very often, when we make personal choices, we try to be original. We do not like to follow a beaten track, whereas in the past it was the opposite—or at least it was what one had to do, and in the case of marriage there was hardly any room for personal choice. At the Council of Trent there was a great debate on whether the authority of parents, and therefore their consent, affected the legitimacy of a marriage. Some French theologians claimed that parents had a right to veto, whereas the Spanish theologians, faithful to Thomas Aquinas, held that parents only had a right to advise, such that, even if they were not in agreement, their children could still be legitimately married. Thus even as early as the Council of Trent the Church defended personal and individual liberty. Saint Thomas had affirmed such freedom of choice, which is practiced most fully within the order of friendship. In friendship, one indeed chooses one's friend, and human friendship reaches a summit with marriage.[194] The grace of marriage is rooted in the freely made choice of the friend, such that if it can be proved that the choice was not freely made then there is no marriage. Every choice of a friend needs to be made freely. It is in the choice that we see what freedom is.

If we want to understand Joseph's freedom and prudence, we need to look at them in the light of the choices that he made, and, to begin with, in the light of his first choice—his choice of Mary. Joseph met Mary and discerned her uniqueness; indeed we could apply to them, in an eminent way, what Saint Thomas says of marriage: *maxima amicitia*, the greatest friendship. The friendship between Joseph and Mary did not, of course, include the gift of the body, and yet there was still "an absolutely true marriage" (*omnino verum*), says Saint Thomas, since it implied the essential perfection of marriage which is the "inseparable union of souls."[195] And we can rightly say that there has never been another human friendship as great as the one that united Joseph and Mary.[196] This is very important, because the meeting between Joseph and Mary, and Joseph's choice of Mary, are decisive events for the divine economy and for the economy of salvation.[197]

This meeting was a very unusual one in that, as we have seen, the tradition of the Church affirms that Mary had totally consecrated herself to God, and done so at a very young age. If Mary had "no knowledge of man" (and had therefore totally consecrated herself to God) yet at the same time was "betrothed to Joseph," then it follows that Joseph, after having accepted Mary's total gift of herself to God, chose to unite himself to Mary to do the will of God.

Mary does not forbid Joseph to love her! The fact that a person is totally given to God does not prevent us from loving him or her; we love that person in the light of his or her consecration to God. Mary responds to Joseph's love with a great intensity of love. If she had "moralized," she would have said, "No, no! I am consecrated to God!" But Mary does not moralize; she is the beloved little child of God, and so there is a greatness to her heart and intelligence that corresponds to the dimensions of God's own. Morality is at the human level; the theological virtues are at God's level. Hence our hearts grow to God's dimensions, thanks to the theological virtues. We know that God is Love and that it is love that makes our hearts grow, and that each time we are lacking in love, our hearts shrink and become hearts of stone, even though a heart of flesh[198] is made to love and to go as far as possible in love.

In trying to understand the choice that Joseph made, we see how great his prudence was. He was not afraid to commit his life to a person so greatly singled out by God as Mary was, because he understood that the more we love God, the more our hearts grow. But what we are talking about is a genuine love for God and not just a little bit of devotion. Little devotions shrink our hearts, whereas charity makes them grow. If God is allowing the current moral delinquency that we see in the world today (for we must call things by their proper name), and if it has increased to an unbelievable degree over the course of this century (and especially within the last twenty years), surely it is to make us discover the greatness of the theological virtues of faith, hope and charity, and to show us that love for God can only make our hearts grow?

In the Old Testament there is an amazing prefiguration that we should often look at, namely, the Covenant between God and Abraham. God speaks to Abraham and asks him to leave everything for His sake. And Abraham does so. But when he has to travel across Egypt, and the situation becomes serious, he says to his wife Sarah, who is still beautiful, "You will say that you are my sister."[199] In other words, "When he sees you, Pharaoh will fall in love with you, because you are beautiful, and since I am your husband he will kill me; so it would be better to say that you are my sister, and thus you will be a link between him and me, and you will have the role of mediator." A beautiful lie, from the point of view of conjugal love! Abraham believes in God and yet he tells this lie! We can see here the gulf that exists between the theological virtues and the moral virtues. Prudence makes us discover this gulf. It also makes us understand that there is no opposition involved, but rather a continuity. However, the theological virtues have requirements which the moral virtues do not. One has to accept being a Christian, and Christians are those "who follow the Lamb wherever He goes."[200] Whatever may be going on at present in the world, God is allowing it to happen; God allows the current ethical and moral disaster. Why? So that we understand better the divine power of the theological virtues, and their greatness. We are sons of God before being perfect men and women, and it is because we are sons of God that we progressively become men and women who tend towards perfection. We tend towards human perfection; we know that we are not yet there, and we must accept setbacks—we must accept all that in the light of faith, hope and charity. The great danger, as we are well aware, is of a "fundamentalist humanism," which would have us be perfect in order to be a child of God. No, this is the opposite of what we see in Scripture. From this point of view, the meeting between Joseph and Mary is extraordinary.

Next comes Joseph's trial: God has come to speak with Mary to ask her consent, and He spoke to her as a husband. We can legitimately use this term, since Scripture tells us that God is Israel's Husband,[201] and the Song of Songs reveals to us the mystery of being espoused to God. As we have seen, Joseph did not doubt the purity of Mary's heart: she could not have deceived him— she loved him too much. But she loved God more than she loved Joseph; she loved Joseph in God. Faced with such an unprecedented situation, what should he do? He should perform an act of humility, an act of extraordinary poverty: accept the will of

God, the will of the Father, over and above his love for Mary: "She is for God and not for me." We may think of him saying to Mary, "You are free; act according to God's gracious will. I was mistaken, but I still love you, and I love you still more because God has chosen you. You are worthy of God; it is to Him that you must belong and not to me." And then the angel comes to Joseph during the night. God rewards him for this heroic act, for this divine prudence: "Take Mary your wife into your home...." Our prudence requires a holy poverty. We need to understand that our human decisions should always be relative to the Father's gracious will for us and for those whom we love, and we should consent to this will by stepping aside.

Let us never forget that, as Saint Thomas Aquinas says, when God allows evil it is always for a greater good. We do not always see it of course, but we do not have to check up on God's action; we can be certain that in every case it is always for a greater good. Faced with all the evil that is currently going on, that God allows, we must have a sufficiently strong hope to be able to say that if God allows it, it must be for something very great, such as a gift of love that we have never yet known. What is it that discourages us? What is it that makes us despair? It is being faced with an evil to which we see no solution: a dead end... At that moment we must say to ourselves that if God has allowed this evil to happen all around us, has allowed all the sufferings that we may know, it is always for a greater good. For Joseph it was not an evil that he faced, but it was still a very great suffering. God could have forewarned him! But He did not, and this was with a view to a greater good for Joseph: so that he would understand better that Mary was a gift for him from God—an unparalleled, royal gift. We do not see this clearly enough. We do not understand nearly enough that the gift of the Virgin Mary in our lives is an extraordinary gift. To have the same mother as Christ!

Continuing to "reread" Joseph's trials from the perspective of prudence would lead us over ground already covered. To finish with, let us just return to the episode in which Joseph's prudence is most clearly revealed. If Joseph is for us the model of prudence, of a prudence that is at once human and divine, he is so in the human choice that he made (for there is no choice more human than a husband's choice of his wife, and Joseph chose Mary without knowing in advance who she was) and also in his fidelity to the Holy Spirit. For it was under the action of the gifts of counsel and of fear of the Lord that he chose Mary and chose her again. The gift of counsel, which puts our intelligence at the service of love, establishes a new order in our activities, an order which is no longer merely that of justice and human prudence, but also that of divine love, of charity. The gift of counsel, assuming prudence without doing away with it,[202] gives us a new lucidity which allows love to be first. The gift of the fear of the Lord (Godly fear),[203] which is at the source of our being poor "in spirit," allows us to understand that one of the most important aspects of our lives is not to block the action of the Holy Spirit upon us and upon those whom we love—in other words, to have that divine courtesy which consists in always allowing the Holy Spirit to take first place, over us and over all our decisions, and in accepting, consequently, to be sometimes left aside (at least apparently so)—to be "the *little ball* of God,"[204] like Saint Thérèse of the Child Jesus.

5

THE "JUST, GOD-FEARING" MAN

The sole personal quality of Joseph that is explicitly revealed to us is that he was "a just man."[205] Scripture reveals this to us in relation to the second choice that Joseph makes with regard to Mary, but in his first choice too, Joseph shows himself to be "just"—the just man *par excellence* of the Old Covenant, for he could not have chosen Mary without having asked God whether this was indeed His will. The "just man," even in the Old Testament, is not the man who is morally perfect; he is not simply someone "who practices the Law,"[206] someone "whose conduct is perfect"[207] in the sense of moral perfection—someone who perfectly accomplishes his duty. He is of course someone who wishes to conduct himself with integrity,[208] but he is also someone who, falling seven times, immediately picks himself up again[209] because he places his trust in God and not in himself:[210]

> If you come forward to serve the Lord, prepare yourself for trials...be patient. For gold is tested in the fire... Trust in [the Lord] and He will help you; make your ways straight, and hope in Him. You who fear the Lord, wait for His mercy...trust in Him, and your reward will not fail.[211]

He who trusts the Lord will not suffer loss. No evil will befall the man who fears the Lord, but in trial He will deliver him again and again.[212]

The truly "just man" of the Old Testament, far from being like the false "just men" such as the Pharisees are, is someone who, like Abraham,[213] "lives by faith"[214] and "fears the Lord";[215] and this fear, far from being the terror evoked by a tyrant, is both "the beginning [the root] of wisdom"[216] and its "fullness" and "crown."[217]

Adoration

We should re-read the Psalms (which Saint Joseph must have prayed with great faith and love) and the book of Sirach to discover more deeply the holiness of the "just, God-fearing man" that Saint Joseph is. This expression is not directly applied to him; we find it used only once in Scripture.[218] But if we read the Old Testament carefully, we can see that the just man is someone who lives fully the requirement implied in "fear of God," that is to say *adoration*, and secondly, (and as a consequence of adoration) humility and *poverty of heart*.[219] The first commandment, the commandment to adore—"You shall worship the Lord your God..."[220]—was expressed in the old Law in terms of "fear" and of "service": "You shall fear the Lord your God; you shall serve Him..."[221] Is adoration not the first "service" that man, in all justice, owes to God? Following Plato and Aristotle, justice has always been defined as "rendering to each his due." Now, the first thing that we owe to God is simply to *be*, to *exist*. In an act of pure love that is absolutely gratuitous (for He is lacking in nothing and I can add nothing to Him), God creates me, creates my spiritual soul; He gives me my being. "What shall I render to the Lord for all His bounty to me?"[222] Surely the first thing is to recognize my total dependence upon Him—a dependence which, far from alienating me, is in fact my greatest dignity.

Joseph must have lived very fervently this first precept of the Law: *adoration*. We can say that he adores already "in spirit and in truth."[223] He is fervent in his adoration, and this develops in him a godly fear—that gift of the Spirit which firstly leads us to adoration, and then becomes, thanks to adoration, a "chaste" rather than servile fear, that is to say, a loving and filial fear.[224]

If the just man of the Old Covenant—and therefore in an eminent way, Joseph—respects God's rights, he also respects the rights of others, and this is not limited to "You shall not kill, you shall not commit adultery, you shall not steal…"[225] etc. The just man of the Old Covenant does more than that; even under the Law he is already compassionate and merciful.[226] But Joseph, as he receives Mary, is the dawn of the New Covenant, and already lives by what Jesus will later reveal to the rich young man: "If you would be perfect [with the perfection of love, which can only come from on high],[227] go, sell what you possess and give to the poor, and you will have treasure in heaven."[228]

Poverty and Humility

As a just man, Joseph therefore has to enter into *poverty*—not only a material poverty, which would probably not have cost him very much, but a poverty of the heart, in all its forms, which accompanies and even enables one to live truly the second commandment, a commandment which is "like" the first: "You shall love your neighbor as yourself."[229] It is love that is mentioned here, but justice towards someone presupposes a love for his person[230]—a love which draws one, beyond the requirements of justice, to the total giving of oneself for the other's sake. Jesus says, "Greater love has no man than this, that a man lay down his life for those whom he loves,"[231] Joseph would have willingly given his life for Mary! But God will, in a certain sense, ask him for more than this. To die physically would probably have been easier for Joseph than the series of "deaths" of the heart that he will live, and which we have already spoken about.

Let us continue our reflection upon this divine "fear" that Joseph lives. This fear, which is a gift of the Spirit, is a loving fear that allows us to keep God's secrets (it is the *gift of fear* that allows us to keep the secrets of God). Joseph, seeing Mary with child, did not for one second doubt her fidelity: He had her word, he knew that she loved him. To doubt the love of someone who has declared his or her love for us is terrible outrage enough (love calls for trust), but to doubt Mary, who had entrusted him with the secret of her total consecration to God, and who had drawn him into this consecration, would have been unthinkable. Totally consecrated to God as she was, Mary did not rely on herself to remain faithful, but rather she relied on God: "Our soul waits for the Lord...we trust in His holy name. May Your steadfast love, O Lord, be upon us, even as we hope in Thee."[232] Joseph will live in his own way this wholly filial fear that Mary has by entering into a new poverty: He offers to God the fervor of his first love, his love for Mary. If such be the will of God, if God is asking that Mary no longer be his betrothed, that she be the virgin who awaits the Messiah,[233] then Joseph will fully accept what God wants. He accepts it in suffering, his heart broken, even though it may be that he does not cry. A young man does not cry very easily (and when one's heart is broken one certainly does not cry; one carries one's suffering interiorly) but still Joseph finds himself totally stripped of everything, in a radical poverty.

God does not set Joseph aside but He does test his heart, to see the extent of his magnanimity,[234] the extent of his faithfulness. Being ready to start everything afresh all over again, saying to God that we are ready to do His will *as He wants* it to be done, and not according to our own little plans, is a radical purification. Joseph had perhaps already made plans after having met Mary, and after she had given him her "yes." In the depths of his heart, and in his human prudence, had he not dreamt of something great and wonderful? All of this must be swept away for him to become poor. It would be impossible to be the husband of Mary and the father of Jesus without being extremely poor. Joseph was certainly not proud, since he was "just and God-fearing," but not being proud and being poor are not the same thing.

Not being proud is the virtue of humility, which is practiced according to our prudence: Joseph stepped aside in this matter regarding Mary because he loved her, and in his prudence he was even happy to step aside for her. We know more or less what constitutes the prudential exercise of humility. Everyday life keeps us humble because in a family, in a group, or in a religious community there is always someone whom we must let take a more important place than ourselves. Sometimes it requires an act of heroism, but all the same, it is a matter of prudence. Prudence requires of us this "normal" humility, which is not yet the poverty of the heart of Jesus.[235] "You will always have the poor with you, but you will not always have Me."[236] The "poor" *par excellence* is Jesus. For Joseph to be able to be the father of Him Who is poor *par excellence*, he had to enter into a very great poverty, and a poverty that he could not speak of to anyone. When poverty touches what is most intimate in our hearts, we cannot talk about it, or at least we can only open up to a very small number of people about it, and in this case we can be sure that Joseph, bound as he was to Mary, could not open up his heart to anyone other than her.

Divine poverty always touches what is most vulnerable in us, because it is the fruit of love, and love is what makes us vulnerable. We are, as it were, skinned alive. We tell the Lord that we could bear any other trial rather than this one. Fortunately, He does not ask us for our opinion. He deliberately targets what is most vulnerable in us—there where we are most capable of loving—

and He does so in order that we become beggars of His heart and so that we are very close to His own poverty. Jesus' poverty is a substantial, radical poverty that places Him in a state of total dependence upon the Word of God, upon the Father, upon the Holy Spirit. It is a poverty that brings Jesus' humanity into the Holy Trinity, and for us, poverty is the "narrow gate"[237] which leads us into the Most Holy Trinity. We can understand, then, why God wanted Joseph, who was to be the father of Jesus, to be so greatly tried.

The Poverty of a Husband and Father

In this trial, Joseph did not simply remain the "just, God-fearing" man that he already was. He went further in faith, hope and love. We could say that, in his faith, he had a presentiment of what had taken place between Mary and her God, a presentiment that God had accomplished something in Mary without asking his permission, without cooperating with him. This is something very hard for a man to accept (it is hard for a woman, too, but perhaps even harder for a man). It is very trying because when we love someone, we have only one desire: to work together with him or her—that that person's work be ours also. Loving Mary as he did, Joseph had a great desire to be able to work together with her. Even though he knew that they would not have any children, since they were not to have conjugal relations, could they not work together on something greater, cooperate on some work of a religious nature, for example? Perhaps that was what Joseph desired? And now, suddenly, everything has fallen apart, and God has acted in a way which has left Joseph out of the picture. How humiliating it is! But this is not what stops Joseph; he does not let himself be beaten by the affective and emotional aspect of the rupture, which is nevertheless very hard indeed. Because he is a "just" man, there is something that is much more important for him, namely, knowing what God's will is for him and what God's will is for Mary.[238] But Mary remains silent... There is only one solution then: to give Mary back to her family.

Joseph's heart is broken by this, but he does not revolt against God. With a great spirit of poverty he accepts this situation of finding himself left aside. A psychoanalyst would say that there is a dreadful suppression here—one of the worst kinds! But no, Joseph fully accepted it because, for him, the Father's will was something far greater than everything else. It was his first encounter with Mary that enabled him to accept it, for if he really accepted the fact that Mary was totally consecrated to God, and that he was to be consecrated also, through Mary (which he did accept), then we can understand that the first thing God requires of him is to go beyond himself in regard to this project— wonderful and great as it may be, the greatest of all human projects—working together with Mary in the spiritual order.

It was indeed the greatest of human projects, but now Joseph must give it up for something greater still, namely, placing himself entirely at the disposal of God's gracious will in a total poverty. Here we touch upon the depths of Joseph's soul: rather than letting himself become hardened when the magnificent project of a spiritual cooperation with Mary falls apart, this man of poverty— this true man of poverty—places himself totally into the hands of his God so that He may do with him what He wills. For Joseph, placing himself into God's hands is exactly that, and it is the consequence of Mary's vow. In accepting Mary's vow, her virginal consecration, Joseph knew that the consequence of this vow is *abandon* in the greatest sense, that is to say, the total gift of oneself to God. Isn't this what every Christian should live? Shouldn't every Christian live by the spirit of the evangelical counsels, since every Christian should live by the spirit of the Beatitudes? The three evangelical counsels of poverty, chastity, and obedience are a kind of "Summary" of the Beatitudes. Every Christian who lives by the spirit of the Beatitudes is led to this attitude of abandon which consists in always letting the will of the Father take precedence—"*Messire Dieu premier servi*" [the Lord God is served first], as Joan of Arc said. We do not seek our own will, our own exaltation and success. We seek *the will of the Father*. This needs to be the sole thing engraved in the depths of our hearts.[239]

In order for this poverty to be complete, God allows several situations which seem only to complicate matters. But in fact, it is very simple: it is God's direct way of making Joseph poor in his fatherhood. He would not have been poor in his fatherhood had he not known this trial, for every fatherhood implies a nuptial love. Without their marriage, without this bond of friendship between Joseph and Mary, there could not have been any fatherhood; it is for this reason that the angel says to Joseph, "Take Mary, your wife." Joseph chose Mary twice: once before his trial and once after his trial. Why? Because God wanted the bond between Joseph and Mary to be wholly divine. We will come back later to the two ways in which charity is exercised in us.[240] In the first link between Joseph and Mary, there is a movement from love of friendship to divine charity, and in the second, from divine charity to love of friendship. It is rare that God makes this double link between two persons. We can easily understand the first one: Joseph chose Mary because he loved her, yet with an absolute respect for God's gracious will for her and for him. The second time, it is God Who tells Joseph to make the choice: "Take Mary as your wife," so this choice comes from on high. Is this not extraordinary? When there is first a friendship love and we enter into God's desire for that friendship, then that is already something beautiful: a human friendship that is purified, divinized. But when it is God Himself Who makes known to us His gracious will, then it is God's choice, a choice of Divine Love, which will "assume" the human love of friendship, and that is something far greater still.

This is always how we can discern whether a friendship is truly divine: if God has preceded our human heart. If God asks us to love someone first in a divine way, in charity, and then later on asks us to love him or her with our human heart and our sensibility, then it is divine love which "assumes" human love. Things are then simpler (even if, in the case of consecrated persons, this requires the total offering which the spirit of virginity calls for), because it is God Who assumes everything. For Joseph and Mary it was both, and it is ultimately for this reason that we can say that there was between them the greatest friendship that ever existed between two creatures; this terrible trial was necessary in order for divine love to be able truly to transform everything from within.

Joseph's fatherhood of the Child Jesus is founded upon this love; for his fatherhood to be wholly divine, this love also had to be wholly divine. When Mary revealed to him that she was totally consecrated to God, Joseph accepted to offer his fatherhood to God. Is this not the greatest offering a young man can make? If God, in His wisdom, wanted man and woman to be the masterpiece of creation, it is with a view to fecundity, and so it is not surprising that this is something so important to us. To offer this fatherhood up to God is to say to Him, not in words but "in deed and in truth,"[241] that our heart wants to love Him in a unique way.

If the greatness of the spirit of virginity lies in the fact that it is totally ordered towards contemplation, as Saint Thomas shows,[242] then it follows that this spirit cannot be lived fully without the desire for contemplation. We can therefore understand that the offering of fatherhood can only be received by God if one has a thirst for contemplation. Otherwise it will always be lived, in various degrees, as something negative, and God does not like that. He does not like us to live in negation, because it is contrary to love. Quite the opposite, we must understand that the offering of fatherhood is for something much greater: to be more immediately bound to God.

Joseph had thus offered up his fatherhood so as to let God be absolutely free with regard to Mary and to himself. And now his trial concerning Mary—that she has conceived a child—obliges him to offer up his love for Mary, the very *foundation* of his fatherhood, which he had not yet offered. Now he must offer it, so as to be poor with the very poverty of Christ. The poverty proper to the Christian life is the complete offering of one's heart, because this is the poverty of Christ, the poverty of Him Who comes to be immolated on the Cross, the poverty of the victim. Such poverty goes a very long way, because it is to accept to be reduced to nothing by the fire of Heaven which comes down upon us, as it did for the sacrifice of Elijah.[243] When one offers oneself to God as a victim of love, as Saint Thérèse of Lisieux did, it is beyond what is human: it is the fire of heaven, the fire of contemplation, the fire of the Holy Spirit, which consumes the victim. Joseph must offer God his human heart, accepting to be alone, for God. And it is at the very moment when he makes this gesture of love, in great solitude, that it is *given* to him, divinely, to be the husband of Mary and the father of Jesus.

We are a little too hasty when we speak of Joseph simply as "foster father." We can see why people call him that, but we need to be careful because there is a risk of diminishing Joseph's fatherhood of Jesus. His fatherhood is a divinely perfect fatherhood wherein the Child Jesus, in all His greatness, nobility and divinity, is relative to Joseph. It is a fatherhood that is substantial, though through grace; it is a fatherhood that requires the sacrifice of not being a human source of life; and it is a fatherhood that requires accepting this poverty in his spousal relationship with Mary. God would not ask for such poverty—this *double* poverty—were it not with a view to a greater love; otherwise God would not be God. He would not be Father. This double poverty is demanded of Joseph so that he be a father with a *divine* fatherhood which is then the reflection in his heart of the Father's unique fatherhood.[244]

6

MAN OF SILENCE, PATRIARCH OF THE MONASTIC LIFE

Scripture does not report a single word spoken by Saint Joseph; we only have his silence. And yet Joseph is not a taciturn man; he is a working man, and all true workers speak very little, because they are fully focused on what they are doing. But more than this, Joseph is a man who is silent in his love—a man who is silent because he loves, and because he lives by a secret, a double secret.

Joseph's Silence

We saw earlier on that Joseph received, one after the other, two secrets from Mary. The first was the secret of her virginal consecration, to which he consented with all his heart; it required him to go beyond himself, inevitably, but it gave him a deep joy. The second secret was that of her divine motherhood, about which he was not consulted in any way.[245] In her silence concerning this secret, Mary showed Joseph that she had an even greater trust in him than she had done with regard to the first secret.[246]

119

Thanks to these two secrets which Mary confided to him, Joseph becomes silent with an *interior* silence. Entering into an interior silence is very difficult. For exterior silence all you need is a little good will—sometimes a rather stoical good will, for one has to educate one's will in order to keep silent. However, interior silence is altogether different: it is not a question of having a stoical will, but rather a question of love, and love implies the communication of secrets.[247] To confide a secret to someone is to show him how much we trust him;[248] the areas of silence within us come from the depth of the secrets we carry. This is true at the simply human level, between friends who are united by a true spiritual friendship (and not just by a passionate or purely emotional love), but it is even more true in the order of grace, when our interior silence comes from the Holy Spirit Who asks us to receive God's secrets and to cooperate with them. Our heart then becomes the place of God's secrets. It is thus that Joseph's heart becomes the place of Mary's secret—the secret of her total consecration to God.

Joseph is a model for us in this respect and has something to teach us. The first way in which Mary teaches Joseph is by telling him her secret, and in so doing by plunging him into silence, because from this moment onwards he is bound to her in a unique way, with a bond brought about by the Holy Spirit Himself. As Saint Thomas says, the Holy Spirit is the *nexus* of the Father and the Son:[249] He is the "knot" or bond in the Most Holy Trinity, and He is also the bond between Mary and Joseph, a bond which plunges Joseph into silence.

Mary will make Joseph's heart blossom so that He can become a true father—a father in such a way that his fatherhood manifests God's own fatherhood of Mary and of us. She who is given to Joseph is she who lives the beatitude of faith,[250] she who bears the Father's treasure—His secret—and who lives from it because the Father has entrusted His Son to her so that He be also *her* son, *her* secret. From this moment onwards, Mary lives an extra-ordinary unity with the Father, Whom we could say, in a certain sense, is there as her Spouse.[251] How deeply Mary must have contemplated the mystery of fatherhood at that moment! During the time she was expecting the birth of her son—the birth of the beloved Son—Mary must have lived, in her contemplation, very intensely this mystery of the paternity of the Father with respect to His Son and with respect to her, since it is through the Father's paternity that she is Mother.[252] There is, then, a unique intimacy between Mary and the Father. Through the Son—the secret of the Father given to her—she lives of the contemplation of the Father; she is hidden in the silence of the Father.

And this is the mystery into which Joseph is introduced: he is to receive the Mother of the Son of God and thus, through her, enter into the paternity of the Father; he is to contemplate it, to understand that it is given to him,[253] and that not only is it given to him in grace—in the depths of his grace—but also that he will have to make it manifest to the human race. He will be, as it were, the "sacrament" of this fatherhood by being the father of Jesus. This will be in a deep poverty, because he knows that his father-hood is wholly divine. It is a fatherhood which is incarnated in his heart, of course, but in a way that implies a great poverty, since Jesus is not the fruit of the fecundity of the union between Joseph and Mary; He is the fruit of the fecundity of Mary united to the Holy Spirit.

Far from making Joseph sad, this great poverty in love intensi-fies his joy:[254] since he loves Mary more than himself, he is happy to step aside for the Holy Spirit. Through the Holy Spirit, she is Mother in a way that reaches a unique perfection: the forming of Christ's body will be more perfect than if it were purely natural. Joseph's great joy is to see himself associated, in complete poverty, with the greatness of Mary's motherhood, which is given to him, and with the greatness of the forming of Christ's body, in which his participation is only divine. How poor Joseph's fatherhood is, and how great!—so utterly selfless, in an unreserved gift of himself, because he loves Jesus and Mary more than himself! We should ask Saint Joseph to reveal to us some small part of what he himself understood of the paternity of God the Father. This is important, because the purpose of the Incarnation is to reveal to us the Father. We should therefore seek to understand the way in which Saint Joseph leads us to the Father.

How is Joseph able to play such an important role in our Christian lives, in our personal lives as children of the Father? Is there not "one mediator between God and men, the man Christ Jesus"?[255] Yes indeed, Jesus is "the mediator of the New Covenant";[256] but, as Saint Thomas is fond of saying, God multiplies His instruments so that His mercy abounds.[257] The Father has no need of any mediator other than His Son in order to reveal Himself, but He wishes to associate Joseph with this work not only as guardian, but also as Jesus' father. This is an entirely gratuitous grace from God. Yet the greater the gratuity of God's love, the more He asks for our cooperation. Hence it is through the poverty of his heart that Joseph will become the one who leads us to the Father, who will be for us the "mediator of contemplation."

How was it that Joseph could become the mediator of contemplation? It was because he offered up his love for Mary, placing it at the disposal of God's good pleasure so that God might do exactly as He willed with her and with him; that's how Joseph becomes the mediator of contemplation. A person has to be very poor in spirit in order to be a mediator of the Kingdom of God. The Kingdom of God is the beatific vision, and thus here on earth it is contemplation. "Blessed are the poor in spirit: theirs is the Kingdom of Heaven."[258] Leading others into contemplation requires a great poverty of heart; without such poverty of heart it is impossible.

Patriarch of the Monastic Life

Marthe Robin[259] used to like to look at the origin of the religious life in Mary, and she emphasized a great deal the necessity of living this first consecration which is brought about in Mary's heart and extended to Joseph's heart. From this perspective, Joseph is truly the patriarch of religious life, of monastic life. He is its patriarch because he kept Mary's secret in silence.[260] The religious life, the monastic life, began in this "underground" way. Isn't this an extraordinary beginning of religious life? The mystery of the Holy Family is what will help us to understand what the renewal of religious life should be, such as the Holy Father is asking for: a renewal of the contemplative life, of a life completely immersed in God—a renewal which takes place through and in the heart of Mary. Of course, the Holy Family remains the model for the Christian family, and even a model for all families, in the quality of the spouses' love and in their fidelity to their responsibility towards their children,[261] but it is not only that. Saint Joseph has also always been considered as the model of authority in the monastic life. The Church gives him to us both as the model of fatherhood in the Christian home and as the model for the exercise of authority in the monastic life. He is the link between flesh-and-blood families and spiritual families—just as Mary is, in fact. This is very beautiful because it shows us that the holiness of the monastic life and the holiness of the Christian household is one and the same holiness; were it not the case, we would have two different models. This is perhaps what we too often forget; we have tended to separate these two sorts of holiness a little too much. Since Canon Law makes a clear distinction between lay people and religious (and at the level of Canon Law it is important to do so), we have placed too great an emphasis upon the external aspects and different rights of temporal families and spiritual families (i.e. the monastic life). We have tended to oppose them rather too much, and have not sufficiently seen their unity.

The great grace of the Second Vatican Council was perhaps to make us discover, or rediscover, the unity that exists between the Christian household and the monastic life, and to show us that there is no separation between the two. There is a distinction, obviously, but a distinction for the purpose of a much deeper unity, because we are all tending towards the same holiness, towards the same intimacy with Christ, with Mary, with Joseph. It is very important that the spirituality of the family today not be separated from monastic spirituality, and that there are profound exchanges in the order of fraternal charity (in the order of *agape*) between Christian households, which are in the world and have temporal responsibilities, and monastic households—spiritual and contemplative households which are totally consecrated to God. The latter remain linked to temporal households and to families, and must help them to go further.

The monastic life, in its most classic and simplest features, is rooted in the life of Joseph, in the silent and hidden life of a worker who worships God and loves Him—a faithful worker, meek and poor. We can apply to Joseph what is said about Moses, the eminent servant to whom God speaks "mouth to mouth"[262] and whose greatest desire is to "see the glory of the Lord":[263] "He sanctified him through faithfulness and meekness; He chose him out of all mankind";[264] "Moses was very meek, more than all the men that were on the face of the earth."[265]

Poor in the work that he did, Joseph accepted that he would not see immediate results. *Faithful*, he ceaselessly offered his work to God, working to the best of his ability yet doing so for God. *Meek*, he did his work without jealousy or rivalry. He worked as a man of poverty, to glorify God. Where did this unceasing concern for God's glory come from? From his faithfulness to adoration. The demands of adoration (which are *interior* and not simply the forced carrying out of a legal recommendation) leave us completely stripped of everything. A man who truly adores considers his work as matter to be consumed in the interior fire of adoration, and he does not expect anything else. Far from being an opposition to prayer or to the contemplative life, work that is lived in this way is a foundation for the monastic life. Monastic work ought to be just that: entirely founded upon adoration, it nourishes our adoration and is completely offered; nothing belongs to us.

What we are talking about here is true for all Christians; for all Christians the fundamental requirement is to live by adoration, "in spirit and in truth" and then, stemming from this adoration, to live by a thirst for contemplation—and to do so in a world in which the utilitarian aspect is so important and where everything is judged according to criteria of efficiency and utility. Faced with this state of affairs, Christians need to affirm, more than ever, the primacy of the gratuity of love. We live by this in adoration, and adoration increases our desire to know God[266]—"And this is eternal life: that they know Thee, the only true God..."[267]—and to contemplate Him, that is, to live by His life.

7

SAINT JOSEPH AND
SAINT JOHN

The two creatures on earth who were closest to Mary were Saint Joseph and Saint John. A comparison between them will help us to penetrate deeper into Mary's heart, since her heart forms the link between them.[268] Saint Joseph *chose* Mary, and Saint John *received* Mary from Jesus.

Joseph was certainly moved by the Holy Spirit (or let us rather say "the Spirit of God" for the "Holy Spirit" as such had not yet been revealed) when he chose Mary to be his wife. But that did not mean that he was prevented from choosing her in a personal and free choice.

It is different for John. He must certainly have already had a deep respect and a true love for the Mother of Jesus, but he would never have dared to "take her into his home." Only an order from Jesus Crucified—"Behold your mother"—meant that he did so. From that moment, John takes her "into his home."[269]

John did not choose Mary. This is a very important point for those who say that they do not have a special devotion to Our Lady. They need to know that John did not choose Mary: it was Jesus Who chose her for him.

Mary's Love for Joseph and for John

When we consider these two men in their relation to Mary, we immediately ask ourselves: which of them did she love more?

We could say that, being immaculate, she loved each of them in a divine way (that is, in charity and in full dependence upon the Holy Spirit) and also in a human way, with great intensity. But there is a difference in that she chose Joseph, or to be more precise she responded to Joseph's choice of her, but this response was still her own personal choice; hence we should not be too quick to say that John holds a more important place than Joseph in Mary's heart. The Church accords Joseph such a privileged position that we must not diminish him by putting John first. Quite the contrary: we should consider Joseph's greatness in all that it is, a greatness that perhaps prepares us for John. But John, who appears later, does not take anything away from the bond which is so strong between Mary and Joseph; for the relationship between John and Mary is different. Mary is given to him as mother, and it is the Woman (Jesus says explicitly, "*Woman*, behold your son"), the woman who is *fully* woman, who is mother. To Joseph is given her youth, but this is not what is given to John. At the Cross, Jesus, the "man of sorrows,"[270] the Lamb of God, gives to John to be his mother she who is "the Bride [or rather the Woman (spouse)] of the Lamb"[271]—the woman of sorrows: "All you who pass by... Look and see if there is any sorrow like my sorrow...."[272] Think of the first time that John looked at Mary... He saw her of course for the first time at Cana,[273] but let us think of the first time that John looked at Mary when Jesus said to him, "Behold your mother." John looked at Mary at that moment, and through her tears he must have seen her smile... For Mary cannot have welcomed John with anything other than a smile, and in silence. She welcomed him through her tears, through her suffering, but a suffering completely transformed by love.

At the time of the Cross, Joseph had already left this world. Mary is present at the Cross, and lives in great unity with Jesus the mystery of the offering of His life to the Father, the offering of His whole self in suffering, rejection and struggle. Mary lives this mystery in her faith, hope and charity; and it is through this mystery of Compassion, at the moment when the prophecy of Simeon is fulfilled—when Mary's heart is "pierced as though by a sword"[274]—that Jesus, looking at His Mother and at His beloved disciple for the last time, says these powerful words to Mary, "Woman, behold your son," and to John, "Behold your mother."[275] This is a new covenant which unites John to Mary in an astonishing and wholly divine way. We can say that, from the moment Jesus speaks these words, John's heart becomes one with the heart of Mary his mother, *just as* Mary's heart becomes one with the heart of Jesus Crucified.

Earlier on we asked whether Joseph or John is more closely united to Mary. Joseph and Mary are intimately bound together; Mary and John are intimately bound together. If we are friends of the Virgin Mary, if we are her children, can we not ask her to reveal her heart to us to show us which of the two she loves more? Some people would say that it's a pointless question, since we cannot know the answer.[276] However, the question still remains; but can we, in fact, answer it? Can we put an order into love? Do we not simply have to say that Mary loves them both, in different ways?

In fact, it is not a trivial or pointless question, for Mary is given also to us to be our mother. Through John, she is given as mother to all who are redeemed by the Cross of Christ; she is given, therefore, to each one of us. And if John wishes to make us live the mystery of his sonship with regard to Mary, then it is our duty to try to understand it as much as we can. In other words, we must discover what it is that the Holy Spirit fashioned between John's heart and Mary's heart. This in turn will enlighten us about

Mary's divine motherhood as it concerns us, and will therefore help us to live her divine motherhood more profoundly.

Mary and John

Let us come back to the words that Jesus addresses to Mary and John—words so intense and so astonishing with which He establishes a new covenant between the beloved disciple and His Mother Mary, whom He gives to the disciple to be his own mother. Jesus addresses each of them in turn, in a certain sense repeating Himself, so as to show that this is indeed a covenant; for, in order for a covenant to exist, the two members of the covenant must be convinced of its reality, so as to be able to live by it.

If John went as far as Golgotha, it was not to find Mary; if he is present at the Cross he is there out of love for Jesus and out of fidelity to Jesus. He is present at the Cross because of his docility to the Holy Spirit. Mary is also present at the Cross on account of her love for Jesus.[277] This is even more understandable and explicit, for she is His Mother—a mother who is faithful and who desires to be faithful right to the very end. The prefiguration in the Second Book of Maccabees[278] of the "admirable mother" can help us to have a better understanding of what takes place at the Cross, and how Mary is there for Jesus, her only son.

At the risk of appearing to shift our focus away from Joseph (although it will in fact help us to understand him better), let us try to penetrate this mystery a little further. Mary is there at the foot of the Cross out of pure love for Jesus; she is also there (and these two things are inseparable) in order to fulfill, to complete in her heart what is lacking in Christ's passion.[279] She is there to receive everything from Jesus, and also to give Him everything—everything that she can give Him through her faith, her hope and her love. Her presence is a presence of love and of gift, because it is a *cooperation* in the mystery of Jesus Crucified. Mary is not a spectator; she is Mother so that she can cooperate with Jesus and live what He lives. She is one with Jesus in her faith, hope and love. She draws her life from Jesus' as she has never done before, with new intensity and new ardor. Completely drawn towards Jesus— "I, when I am lifted up from the earth, will draw all men to myself"[280]—she is one with Him in offering everything that she has and everything that she desires to have. Everything is offered, everything is given. In her faith, hope and love, she lives everything that Jesus lives in a perfect, "quasi-infinite" love,[281] going beyond all obstacles and beyond everything that could limit this love.

Christ Himself enjoys the beatific vision from the very first moment of His Incarnation.[282] We must therefore affirm that when He is living the mystery of the Cross the heights of His intelligence remain immersed in the light of the beatific vision, and the heights of His will remain immersed in the love of the Trinity.[283] There is something within Christ's soul which cannot be offered up as a victim, cannot be consumed to the point of disappearing like the victim of a holocaust. Saint Augustine calls this the "superior part"[284] of Christ's soul, which remains always in glory. There is, then, a part of Christ's sacred humanity which does not take part in His victimal state, and this is why Mary offers herself with Him, so that in her what is most profound in the human will and intelligence might be offered to God. And Mary's wholly divine cooperation, this unity between them, is a source of happiness for Jesus. So that the victim be perfect, so that humanity be completely offered to God, it was necessary that Mary unite herself to the sacrifice of her beloved Son, and that she live the same mystery *in faith*, in which her intelligence was entirely offered to God. Thanks to Mary, the human intelligence was offered as a the victim of a holocaust at the Cross, and it is there that Mary lives the beatitude of faith: "Blessed is she who believed...."[285]

We can experience something of this when God asks us to live certain sufferings that we do not understand—sufferings in our heart or in our intelligence. We can be tempted to think that He is making us suffer simply for the sake of it, gratuitously and for no apparent reason: we could have explained things better to that other person, we could have tried to understand each other... But no, there is total darkness. We cannot see anything, we cannot understand anything, and yet we continue to live, thanks to love. This is what Mary lived at the Cross, so that the mystery of Christ's offering might fully encompass the human intelligence. And we can say the same about her will: all of the desires of Mary's heart, human desires transformed by grace (hence desires that were good, noble and great), had to be offered and consumed, in hope. In this, Mary lives the beatitude of those who hunger and thirst, and the beatitude of the pure of heart, and the beatitude of the poor...

At the very moment when Mary becomes one with Him, Jesus asks her to look at John, and gives her to John. Mary had only one desire: to look at Jesus, to be totally dependent on Jesus, to be with Him, lost in Him—and He asks her to look at John. She passes from contemplation to fraternal charity and mercy (for accepting to be John's mother was a great act of mercy on her part). To be "one" with Jesus in the mystery of the Cross is the greatest contemplation that can exist, and Mary lives it; but now, through this contemplation, she lives a new requirement of charity, accepting to be, as it were, set to one side in order to go further in love, and to live a deeper holocaust. This suffering is lived in love, and thus in joy, but it is still a suffering, for everything is taken away from her—everything. Jesus had to accept being stripped of His clothing,[286] and yet that was nothing compared to the interior stripping in which He gives away His mother, drawing her into this same naked poverty, because He wants her to belong entirely to John, to the Church and to each one of us. We see here an infinitely noble will of Christ in which His Heart is completely stripped of everything: she who has been given to Him by the Father, and who is now one with Him in this joint work, is given to John so that he understand both how much Jesus loves him, and that he must belong entirely to Mary to belong entirely to Jesus. Far from separating him from Jesus, Mary will enable John to be more closely united to Him. Jesus' words, which seem to cause a separation, actually bring about an even deeper unity between the hearts of John and Jesus, and between the hearts of Mary and Jesus. This is the great mystery of the fruitfulness of the Cross which comes to us through Mary's love for John. Mary, completely saved by a pure gift of love (she is immaculate), manifests to the whole world the admirable fruitfulness of the Cross,[287] of Christ's holocaust, and she also manifests this fruitfulness through her divine motherhood of John; the two go together.

Mary's love for John is indeed unique. It is a mystery—the mystery of fraternal charity in its most eminent and perfect aspects, through and in the mystery of the Cross. Only the Cross can enable us to grasp Mary's love for John and for us.

The Two Ways We Exercise Fraternal Charity

Hence we see that we may indeed ask how we are to understand the bond between Mary and Joseph in comparison to the bond between Mary and John. It is clear that there is no rivalry involved, but these two different loves do help us to understand Mary's heart—a radiant heart, burning with love. Her love for Joseph and her love for John reveal to us, each in their own way, how much Mary loves Jesus, for her love for Joseph and her love for John stem from her unique love for Jesus, for her God. That is why it is helpful to look at these two different links, so that through them we may discover the unique bond that Mary had with Jesus—a bond from which this double love, for Joseph and for John, springs forth.

If we compare these two relationships of love—as far as they may be compared—we see that Mary's divine love for Joseph "assumes" the human love of a wife for her husband, and that this human love is entirely transformed through charity. It is different in John's case. Undoubtedly, before Calvary, Mary loved John with a love of charity, but we cannot say that humanly speaking she had chosen him in a special way before the Cross. She had surely guessed how much Jesus loved John, and because of that, was probably more attentive to him. But we cannot definitively say anything about it because it is not something we are told about; we simply do not know. We do know, however, about the supernatural request that Jesus Himself makes of Mary concerning John: "Woman, behold your son," repeated when He addresses John: "Behold your mother." Here is a love that is entirely divine; it becomes incarnate, of course, and will continue to become more and more incarnate right up to the end of Mary's earthly life, but it remains first and foremost a divine love.

It would be very interesting to look into this more deeply in theology, for this is where we see the two ways in which charity—supernatural love—may be exercised in us. Either charity "assumes" an already existing (or simultaneously existing) human friendship, or else the mystery of divine charity comes first and is then incarnated in our human capacity to love, and thus in a human love. It always happens in one of these two ways in our lives: either charity "assumes" human friendships, transforming them, or alternatively, the bonds of charity which God forms become the source of an incarnation that gives rise to a human love and then sustains it.[288] Then the whole human being is transformed by divine love, allowing our relationships of charity to have a unique strength and intensity.

This is what happens for Mary. From this perspective, it is wonderful to understand that the love she has for Joseph is entirely ordered towards the love she has for the mystery of the Word Incarnate, and that all her love for John stems from her divine, supernatural love for Jesus. "Love one another *as* I have loved you":[289] Mary is to love John with that love. We must not forget that our fraternal charity is the extension of this ultimate covenant which was realized between Mary and John at the Cross. After He has instituted the Eucharist and given Himself to His Apostles as food, Jesus gives them this new commandment: "*As* I have loved you, love one another." Jesus put this precept into practice in an eminent way on the Cross, when He said to Mary, "Woman, behold your son," and to John, "Behold your mother." At its very summit, fraternal charity takes on this maternal form.

Fraternal charity between Mary and Joseph has a very different form: they are husband and wife, whereas Mary and John are mother and child (John is her beloved child because he is the beloved disciple, and Mary is to love him *as* Jesus has loved him). We have here, therefore, on the one hand a fraternal charity rooted in a human friendship, and on the other a fraternal charity rooted in contemplation, the contemplation of the Cross. If Mary is united to John so closely it is because she lived with him the contemplation of the wisdom of the Cross, the contemplation of Jesus Crucified. This is the foundation of their charity, and here charity reaches a summit.

It is difficult to know whether Mary's fraternal charity towards Joseph is greater or lesser than it is towards John. What we can say for certain is that the fraternal charity which unites Mary to John has a more perfect *"divine" mode*, because it is more contemplative, whereas her fraternal charity towards Joseph is more perfectly *rooted*. In the eyes of God, each of these fraternal charities is unique, and both are *models* for us: a model of fraternal charity in the Christian home (Joseph), and in the religious, and especially the monastic, life (John).

We need to ask Mary often to teach us to live this mystery of divine charity which progressively transforms all that we are, and especially our heart, so that our love for Jesus becomes the source of every love that is born in our hearts. And if we have bonds with those whom we love which precede this mystery of charity, then we must ask the Holy Spirit to transform those bonds, to "divinize" them by impoverishing them, so as gradually to make more room in us for a divine love that becomes incarnate.

The Old Covenant Brought to Completion

Let us now come back to Joseph. His betrothal to Mary had a particular character to it, for she could not have been betrothed to him unless she had confided to him the total gift of herself to God—otherwise the betrothal would not have been "valid," as we said above.[290] And Mary herself could not have agreed to this engagement and to this marriage without drawing Joseph with her into this gift. In this sense, Joseph is, as it were, the first of her spiritual children...

Joseph loved Mary as no other man on earth has ever loved a woman, as no husband ever loved his wife. He loved her *madly*.[291] The meeting between Jacob and Rachel,[292] which is so beautiful and pure, tells us something about the meeting between Joseph and Mary. Jacob was seized by Rachel's presence, by her gaze. He is captivated by her, and from that moment onwards he is a different man. There is a prefiguration here. Mary probably also used to go to draw water from the well... In Nazareth the fountain where Mary would have gone to fetch water is venerated; nothing tells us that Joseph met her there, but what we can be sure of is that Joseph's first meeting with Mary must have been a very great moment. And since it is the *person* that one encounters, Mary could not have hidden her bond with God from Joseph, for it was the most personal thing about her. Joseph received Mary's secret and entered into it fully, and from this moment onwards he is united to Mary's heart in a love that is one of a divine choice.

The whole of the Old Covenant reaches its fulfillment in this secret covenant between Joseph and Mary. Joseph agrees to be officially Mary's husband, whilst offering his life together with her for the glory of God, and to hasten the hour of the redemptive Incarnation.

Let us look at this in more detail for a moment: the Old Covenant reaches its fulfillment in Mary's heart, in her total consecration to God. This is what she is *capable* of doing. The mystery of her motherhood is an absolutely gratuitous grace, but what she is capable of doing is offering herself to God by consecrating herself to Him; later, she will offer to God her human love for Joseph, an offering which will bring to a close the great awaiting of the Old Testament. When Mary met Joseph, she could have said, "Yes, I consecrated myself to God... But I made a mistake." Joseph was so great! He was certainly the best amongst all his peers... He was the one most loved by God. Mary's meeting with Joseph could have been an obstacle; indeed it was something so "out of the ordinary" that Joseph has almost always been represented as an old man. But Joseph truly chose Mary as his *wife*, and receiving her secret he agreed to follow her in her consecration to God, and so to consecrate himself fully to God also. In this way, the family opens out onto the religious life, and the very first religious community is the ultimate moment for the family.

So, their meeting took place and the result is that Joseph weds himself to Mary's secret—her consecration to God—and in espousing her secret he is united to her so as to be the guardian of her virginity, and, later on, the guardian of her divine motherhood. How great is this ending of the Old Covenant and beginning of the New!

The bond between Mary and Joseph is entirely ordered towards the mystery of the Word "made flesh"[293] within Mary, towards the mystery of the Incarnation. According to the order of God's wisdom, it was necessary that Mary be totally consecrated to God, and that this consecration be the source of Joseph's own consecration.

Here God takes up again the beginning of Genesis: Eve had drawn Adam into eating the forbidden fruit, so as not to be alone. Now Mary, guided by the Holy Spirit, consecrates herself body and soul to God and draws Joseph into this total consecration. And in Mary and Joseph, consecrated in this way, humanity will receive the mystery of the Incarnation. It is Mary, of course, who receives it first of all, but Joseph, guardian of the Virgin and Mother, becomes a father in a totally virginal fatherhood, but one which is nonetheless a true fatherhood.

God requires of each of them this total gift, this total surrender to His gracious will, and He makes use of the love that unites them in order to "visit"[294] mankind, to come *into* mankind through the mystery of the Incarnation—"The Word became flesh and pitched His tent among us, in us."[295] In Mary and Joseph, who are united inseparably, virginity becomes divinely fruitful; here the awaiting of the Old Covenant is brought to a close and here the New Covenant begins. In order for this to happen, there *needed* to be a man who, with a perfect love, would agree to hide the mystery from the eyes of men by being the guardian of the Virgin Mother and of the Child. This is how Joseph cooperates in the Incarnation. According to the plan of God's wisdom, it was *necessary* that Joseph meet Mary and wed himself to her secret, making it his own, so that the mystery of the Incarnation of the Word within Mary might remain hidden. Joseph's role was to hide Mary and Jesus—He Who will be called "the son of Joseph,"[296] "the carpenter's son."[297] And once Joseph has left this world,[298] it will be Jesus Who keeps Mary hidden; we see this from the Gospels, where she is so little mentioned[299] and where, from the Wedding Feast at Cana up until the Cross, no words of Jesus are addressed explicitly to her.

However, at the Cross, as at Cana, Jesus does address Mary, calling her "Woman," and He does so in order to bring about a second covenant, this time with John. There is an order between these two covenants—Mary and Joseph, Mary and John. The first one is the covenant of husband and wife, in a great mystery of gift and in an extreme poverty. Joseph must have needed a great poverty to have been able to live by the mystery of Mary and to keep her hidden! "To let people believe that…"—that's not easy for a man! It was not a lie, of course, nor should we call it a "camouflage." But still, in the eyes of the world, he was Jesus' father… This is how Joseph enters into the secrets of God, being put to one side, in a certain sense, so that the spiritual and the divine take hold of everything in him. Such poverty, and yet such greatness! He must let divine friendship take everything, and must hide Mary accepting all the while that people will believe him to be her true husband. He is of course her true husband, but in a completely different way from the way people imagine. The *maxima amicitia* which Saint Thomas speak about—"the greatest of friendships"—is a nuptial friendship in the eyes of men, and in the eyes of God is a total gift of self which allows His work to be accomplished within Mary. Joseph's greatness lies in the fact that he carries this secret in such a way as to keep it hidden.

As for the second covenant, realized by Jesus at the Cross between John and Mary, it is a covenant between son and mother, as we have already seen. We can thus say that the Old Covenant is brought to its completion in the covenant of husband and wife—yet requiring of them the poverty that they love one another even while agreeing to offer each other totally to God, in their hearts and in their flesh (the Old Covenant is brought to completion in this offering of their virginity)—and that the New Covenant begins with a mystery of motherhood and sonship. This should shed some light for us on the link between the Old Covenant and the New. Mary brings the Old Covenant to completion, and begins the New; thus it is the Woman who brings to fulfillment the Old Covenant (the man, Joseph, being relative to her), and it is she who begins the New Covenant through her motherhood, with the man (John) becoming henceforth her child, in the poverty of evangelical littleness.

Mary and Joseph

Mary, Joseph and John are like three great reflections of Jesus, but there is a certain order to them because, in Mary, the reflection of Jesus is supreme and primary, since she is immaculate. We cannot say that Joseph is immaculate. Some theologians have wanted to proclaim the immaculate conception of Saint Joseph, but the Church has not said anything which would authorize us to do so, and we have to uphold Joseph's very great humility. That does not mean, of course, that an immaculate conception does away with humility! But we must maintain this very hidden mystery of Joseph, the silence that he lived and which enveloped him.

We cannot separate these two men who are so closely united to the Virgin Mary—Joseph and John. But here we are looking at Mary and Joseph, and we need to seek to understand what it is that we should ask of each of them.

Of Mary we ask for the most intimate secrets of Jesus' heart; she is the "good soil,"[300] the Father's beloved, she who "comes up from the wilderness, leaning upon her beloved,"[301] that is, on the Father, on Jesus and on the Holy Spirit. Mary comes up from the wilderness leaning on her Beloved in the joyful mysteries, the sorrowful mysteries and the glorious mysteries. She is the bride of the Father, the bride of the priestly heart of Jesus and the bride of the Holy Spirit. We need to uphold all three; even if nowadays the last aspect is emphasized more than the others, we still have to uphold all three. Saint Thomas sees Mary as the bride of the Father[302] from the moment of the Annunciation when she receives the Father's secret. At the Cross she is the bride of the priestly heart of Jesus; she is the *socia*, as Saint Albert the Great says, the one who is "associated," who cooperates and who completes. And we can also say that, for the Church, she is the bride of the Holy Spirit. Saint Louis-Marie Grignon de Montfort and Fr. Kolbe both insist on that very strongly.[303]

Mary fashions our heart into a virginally clear and pure heart, since in her, *through hope*, we are already immaculate.[304] She fashions in us a heart which knows no lie or guile. A woman who is truly a woman always cares a great deal about loyalty, and man needs woman: "It is not good for man to be alone."[305] Mary is given to us, and it is very important that we understand the particular atmosphere that Mary brings to our hearts: an atmosphere of gentleness, of thirst for love and of great simplicity. Mary introduces us to the mystery of silent prayer and to the mystery of contemplation.

Joseph is given to us, through Mary, in a way that is wholly interior. The Gospel does not reveal any act by which Mary gives Joseph to us, but we know that everything that belongs to Mary belongs to us, because she is our Mother. So she even gives us Joseph, and the fact that she gives him to us is perhaps one of Mary's great secrets, because he is indeed the man who is her earthly husband and thus the spouse of her sensibility and of her womanly heart. He is her guardian, he is entrusted with her fragility, he is responsible for the Woman in whom is accomplished the masterpiece of all Creation. In theology, we can indeed say that Mary is the measure and the keystone of all Creation, and Joseph is the guardian of this masterpiece of God. Mary's body, the body of the Woman who is the object of a unique predilection on the part of God, is the temple of the Holy Spirit in an eminent way. If Saint Paul is able to say of each one of us that "our body is the temple of the Holy Spirit,"[306] this is even truer of Mary, the Woman who guards God's secrets, because she received in herself the Secret of the Father: the Word made flesh. Mary's body, the temple of the Holy Spirit, this body which is at one and the same time so sensitive, so pure and so strong, is given to Joseph. Is this not extraordinary? God could very well have jealously kept Mary all to Himself, and that would have been quite right. She would have been God's hermit... And it is true, Mary *is* the hermit *par excellence*, the solitary one *par excellence*.

God could have had Mary withdraw into the desert. She would have asked a faithful and vigorous man—a Joseph—to build her a little hermitage in the desert, and she could have asked Joseph to build another hermitage not too far from her own so that he could be her guardian. Isn't that what we would have done? But it is not what God did. He wanted Mary to live in Joseph's home, and Joseph to live with Mary, to be her husband, and, as her husband, to be her guardian. There are different ways of guarding: one can be a guardian from the outside or from the inside. Joseph guards Mary as a husband. He is the husband of God's treasure, of her who is the masterpiece of both Creation and of the re-creation, of grace... God *gave* her to him. Joseph chose her, of course, and his greatness lies in his doing so. But having chosen her in a human way, he had to choose her and then re-choose her in a divine way—as a gift from God requiring a purification of the human friendship that already existed between them, great as it was.

This radical purification of the heart is certainly one of the things that we should ask Saint Joseph for the most. It will undoubtedly draw us a long way into poverty, since it will require the offering of all of our human capacities for loving... but we also know (and Saint Joseph shows us this very clearly) that, at the very moment when we offer everything, God gives everything back to us. But that does not mean that we should offer things up so that God gives them back! That would not be a pure offering. We should make our offerings in the same way that Joseph did. We must ask him to teach us to offer what is most precious in our hearts. Joseph is the one who radically purifies our hearts, who requires every love which is born in our hearts to be offered to God. If we do not do this, then we do not love as the Holy Spirit wants us to love. But if we do do it (and usually we have to do it several times) then the Holy Spirit can take possession of our hearts, and God can do this wonderful thing: He can give us back our first love in an even greater way than before. The angel tells Joseph that he not only *can* but that he *must* take Mary into his home; his love for Mary fully conforms to the Father's will, and this love is to develop and blossom.

We must ask Joseph, with his purity of heart, to give us his *poverty* and his sense of the *gratuity* of God's love.

Why does God make us poor? Because He wants to hollow out great desires in us (this is where we discover the meaning of all of our great trials) and He wants us to become capable of receiving His love without holding on to it possessively. For we hold on to God's gifts, and as soon as we hold on to them as something we own, they are no longer God's gifts: they are reduced to our own size. We keep hold of them and make them relative to ourselves, and this making them relative to ourselves means that they are no longer something according to God's dimensions but according to our own. So they are therefore no longer God's gift. This instinct for making things our very own is terrible, and it is perhaps what is most deep-rooted in us from the psychological perspective, i.e. from the perspective of the consequences of original sin: we are beings who want to make things our very own. As soon as we love someone we say that he or she is "*my* good!" But that's not true at all! Yes, of course, since we love that person, he or she is a good for us,[307] but a good that is given to us gratuitously and that requires us not to be possessive. A great purification of the heart is needed for us to manage to live the gratuity of love. Joseph is a man of gratuity. God marked him deeply in this way so that he could receive Mary gratuitously and live with her in this gratuity; it is thus that he became the husband of Mary and the father of Jesus.

How did God prepare Joseph's heart for this? Through *adoration* and *work*. Through adoration and through work, God prepares us for an "*invasion*" of love, and to be able to love always more. For we never love enough. We can never say, "*Now* I love; now I am living the gratuity of love." If we say that, then it proves that we have not truly entered into the gratuity of love, for if we had entered into it we would realize that we always fall short of what we should be doing.

What is it then that prepares us to live this gratuity of love? What is it that prepares us to love and that enlarges our heart so that we can love truly, following Joseph's example? It is *adoration*—the first commandment[308]—and *work*. These are the two great sources of purification from selfishness, from pride, from all the consequences of sin that we carry.

Joseph is the man of adoration and of work.[309] These are *means*. The *end* is love—love for Mary and, through her, love for Jesus. Mary is truly she who leads Joseph to Jesus, and for each one of us Mary plays this same role. It is Jesus Who gives Mary to John—and to us—but in Joseph's case we can say that it is Mary who gives Jesus to him. Only Mary could give Jesus to Joseph; she was carrying Him within her. Joseph chose Mary, and in choosing her, he receives Jesus. So it is then right to say that we go to Jesus through Mary; it is eminently true for Joseph, and Joseph's role is to help us discover this. As for John, he receives Mary from Jesus, and he lives in the intimacy of Mary's heart through the action of the Holy Spirit.

The mystery of Mary is given to us gratuitously, and for John it is an astounding gratuity, even though he was disposed to it by his faithfulness to Jesus. Had John not been faithful unto the Cross, he would not have received Mary. It is owing to his fidelity—following the Lamb wherever He goes, as far as the Cross—that John receives Mary. And we can say the same thing for Joseph: it is thanks to his faithfulness to God his Father (faithfulness in adoration and work) that his heart is disposed to look at Mary, to come to know her and to love her. How wonderful this is: two saints so well-disposed, each of them, to meeting Mary! Mary is given to us too, gratuitously, but let us never forget that God likes to reward faithfulness. That's why He desires us to dispose ourselves well to receiving Mary through a faithfulness similar both to John's and to Joseph's—two extreme forms of faithfulness. Joseph's is a faithfulness in work and in adoration; this is the fidelity of the monastic life, a fidelity that is humble, hidden, unseen by the world (we do not know anything about Joseph's life before he is introduced as being betrothed to Mary). John's faithfulness is very different, since it is first of all a personal bond with Jesus—a personal bond which leads him all the way to the Cross. Yet the fruit of each of their fidelities is to be able to receive Mary into the depths of their hearts. It is different for each of them; it is entirely different at the psychological level, but on the divine level it is the same substantial love, which takes on two different yet complementary forms.

It is important to look at how these two men see Mary. We must ask Saint John to teach us to see Mary just as he did when he heard Jesus say to her, "Woman, behold your son," and then immediately afterwards heard Jesus say to him, "Behold your mother." John's heart was changed into the heart of a child of

Mary; something new was born within him. And in Joseph's heart, too, something new was born when the angel said to him, "Do not be afraid to take Mary your wife into your home ...."[310] For a theology of fraternal charity, it is important to understand these two great ways in which charity takes hold of our hearts, with Saint Joseph as our model on one side and Saint John as our model on the other.

APPENDIX

THE PLACE OF SAINT JOSEPH IN THE ECONOMY OF SALVATION[1]

The special motives for which Saint Joseph has been pro-claimed Patron of the Church, and from which the Church looks for singular benefit from his patronage and protection, are that Joseph was the spouse of Mary and that he was reputed the father of Jesus Christ. From these sources have sprung his dignity, his holiness, his glory. In truth, the dignity of the Mother of God is so lofty that naught created can rank above it. But as Joseph has been united to the Blessed Virgin by the ties of marriage, it may not be doubted that he approached nearer than any to the eminent dignity by which the Mother of God surpasses so nobly all created natures. For marriage is the most intimate of all unions which from its essence imparts a community of gifts between those that by it are joined together. Thus in giving Joseph the Blessed Virgin as spouse, God appointed him to be not only her life's companion, the witness of her maidenhood, the protector of her honor, but also, by virtue of the conjugal tie, a participator in her sublime dignity. And Joseph shines among all mankind by the most august dignity, since by divine will, he was the guardian of the Son of God and reputed as His father among men. Hence

[1] Extract from Leo XIII's encyclical, *Quamquam pluries* (1889).

it came about that the Word of God was humbly subject to Joseph, that He obeyed him, and that He rendered to him all those offices that children are bound to render to their parents. From this twofold dignity flowed the obligation which nature lays upon the head of families, so that Joseph became the guardian, the administrator, and the legal defender of the divine house whose chief he was. And during the whole course of his life he fulfilled those charges and those duties. He set himself to protect with a mighty love and a daily solicitude his spouse and the Divine Infant; regularly by his work he earned what was necessary for the one and the other for nourishment and clothing; he guarded from death the Child threatened by a monarch's jealousy, and found for Him a refuge; in the miseries of the journey and in the bitternesses of exile he was ever the companion, the assistance, and the upholder of the Virgin and of Jesus. Now the divine house which Joseph ruled with the authority of a father, contained within its limits the scarce-born Church. From the same fact that the most holy Virgin is the mother of Jesus Christ is she the mother of all Christians whom she bore on Mount Calvary amid the supreme throes of the Redemption; Jesus Christ is, in a manner, the first-born of Christians, who by the adoption and Redemption are His brothers. And for such reasons the Blessed Patriarch looks upon the multitude of Christians who make up the Church as confided specially to his trust—this limitless family spread over the earth, over which, because he is the spouse of Mary and the Father of Jesus Christ he holds, as it were, a paternal authority. It is, then, natural and worthy that as the Blessed Joseph ministered to all the needs of the family at Nazareth and girt it about with his protection, he should now cover with the cloak of his heavenly patronage and defend the Church of Jesus Christ.

Litany of Saint Joseph

Lord, have mercy.	*Lord have mercy.*
Christ, have mercy.	*Christ have mercy.*
Lord, have mercy.	*Lord have mercy.*
Christ, hear us.	*Christ graciously hear us.*
God the Father of Heaven,	*Have mercy on us.*
God the Son, Redeemer of the world,	*Have mercy on us.*
God the Holy Spirit,	*Have mercy on us.*
Holy Trinity, one God,	*Have mercy on us.*
Holy Mary,	*Pray for us.*
Saint Joseph,	*Pray for us.*
Noble Son of David,	*Pray for us.*
Splendor of Patriarchs,	*Pray for us.*
Spouse of the Mother of God,	*Pray for us.*
Chaste protector of the Virgin,	*Pray for us.*
Foster-father of the Son of God,	*Pray for us.*
Zealous defender of Christ,	*Pray for us.*
Head of the Holy Family,	*Pray for us.*
Joseph most just,	*Pray for us.*
Joseph most pure,	*Pray for us.*
Joseph most prudent,	*Pray for us.*
Joseph most courageous,	*Pray for us.*
Joseph most obedient,	*Pray for us.*
Joseph most faithful,	*Pray for us.*

Mirror of patience,	*Pray for us.*
Lover of poverty,	*Pray for us.*
Model of workmen,	*Pray for us.*
Glory of domestic life,	*Pray for us.*
Guardian of virgins,	*Pray for us.*
Mainstay of families,	*Pray for us.*
Comfort of the afflicted,	*Pray for us.*
Hope of the sick,	*Pray for us.*
Patron of the dying,	*Pray for us.*
Terror of demons,	*Pray for us.*
Protector of the Holy Church,	*Pray for us.*

Lamb of God, Who take away the sins of the world,
Spare us, O Lord.

Lamb of God, Who take away the sins of the world,
Graciously hear us, O Lord.

Lamb of God, Who take away the sins of the world,
Have mercy on us.

℣. He has made him master of His house,
℟. And the ruler of His possessions.

LET US PRAY: O God Who, in Your loving providence, chose Blessed Joseph to be the spouse of Your most Holy Mother, grant us the favor of having him for our intercessor in Heaven whom on earth we venerate as our Protector. You, Who live and reign forever and ever. Amen.

Prayers to Saint Joseph

Prayer of Saint Francis de Sales

Glorious Saint Joseph, spouse of the Virgin Mary, we beseech you through the heart of Jesus Christ, grant to us your fatherly protection.

O you whose power reaches all our necessities and knows how to make possible the most impossible things, open your fatherly eyes to the needs of your children. In the confusion and pain which press upon us, we have recourse to you with confidence.

Deign to take beneath your charitable guidance this important and difficult affair, cause of our worries, and make that its happy outcome serve for the glory of God and the good of His devoted servants. Amen.

Prayers from Saint Joseph's Oratory
Montreal, Quebec[311]

Model of Laborers

Good Saint Joseph, when God wanted a family for His Son, He looked among the laborers, and chose you along with Mary, demonstrating His esteem for human work. You put your heart into your work, and share your workshop with Jesus. Your work, like that of other humans, found new meaning in the presence of God.

Sustain us in the hope of finding work when we are confronted with the desolation of unemployment. Counsel business leaders to create an equitable division of labor that is respectful of individuals, and promotes our growth and happiness. Help us to perform our work joyfully, conscientiously, fairly and honestly. Prepare our hearts to recognize your Son in our colleagues at work. Amen.

Joseph, Guardian of the Pure in Heart

Gentle Joseph, God is captivated by the quality of your heart. Your entire being is focused on doing His will. With Mary and Jesus, you answer the Holy Spirit's call to build a better world.

With one heart, we join you in saying: *"Here we are, Lord, Your will be done! Your kingdom come nearer to us!"*

Keep the hope of a new world alive in our hearts. Inspire us to speak words of tenderness to awaken the love of hearts.

May we draw the energy for our actions from the source of all Love so our faces may shine with the freedom of the children of God. Amen.

Joseph, Mainstay of Families

Attentive Joseph, in Mary and you, the Divine Word finds a favorable environment in which to carry out the will of the Father; thus, you become the family of the Child-God.

In your gentle life together, you experience Love daily. The unity of your hearts transforms life's lessons into growing wisdom and grace. Open our hearts to the Word that lives within us, that our actions may bear witness to our connection to the family of God.

Sustain us in our emotional commitments, where giving and forgiveness shape our identities. Grant us your tenderness in the things we do each day! Amen.

Comfort of the Afflicted

Compassionate Joseph, one with us in our human condition, together with Mary and Jesus you experience exile, hunger and violence. Refusing vengeance, you choose mercy. Your forgiveness breaks the circle of violence. Through your goodness, God's hope for our humanity is preserved. Joy is yours, for the Kingdom of God is your inheritance.

Open our compassionate hands in times of war, famine and exile. Keep us from developing a victim's mentality, and make our pain a source of growth. Sustain us in fulfilling our responsibility of cultivating inner peace, joy and serenity. In your wisdom, counsel us to close all doors to bitterness, so that, watched over by God, we may dance for joy. Amen

Hope of the Sick

Benevolent Joseph, the Son of God placed His life in your hands. With Mary, you cared for Him Who is the force of life. May your compassion enfold our fragility, bringing us the comfort of the divine presence.

We join with you in prayer, saying: *"Lord Jesus, Son of Living God, say a word for our healing!"* Make us sensitive to the illnesses of those close to us. Support our efforts and grant us courage in the fight against all evil.

Help us to find meaning in God's great project for humanity beyond the sicknesses and sufferings that blind our sight. The love of God be with us, as our hope lies with Him! Amen.

Patron of the Dying

Faithful Joseph, with the fulfillment of the Lord's promise, you peacefully leave this world in Jesus and Mary's hands. Your faith transforms death into the sowing of life; thus, God considers you to be a just man. Your heart overflows in the presence of the Lord.

With your hands outstretched to God, your night is filled with prayers. Surrounded by the living, you embark upon the great march to the promised Land.

Open our eyes that we may glimpse the road to Life that lies beyond death. May nothing, not denial, anger, nor depression, separate us from the Love of God. Strengthen our faith in God Who always finds ways of preserving us in His friendship. Be beside us to hold our hands when we take our first steps toward the Eternal Kingdom. Amen.

Protector of the Church

Brave Joseph, collaborator in God's project for humanity, your tenderness enfolds the newborn Church. Just as Mary and Jesus recognize in you the protection of the Father, so too does the community of faith place itself under your protection.

Strengthen us with the Spirit that filled the Nazarene home and guide our footsteps on the road to the Kingdom. Accompany us in carrying out our mission. Help us to be lights in the world so that the family of God may spring forth from humanity transfigured in Christ.

Grant us the strength to imitate God's preference for the poor and weak. Guide us in our pastoral activities that our actions may be modeled on the Good News. Amen.

Notes

Part One: The Mystery of Joseph

1. Mt 1:19.

2. Mt 1:1.

3. Mt 1:16.

4. Lk 3:38. In the genealogy given by Luke, Abraham is considered only in passing, as but one figure in the procession going back to Adam, who is the first origin.

5. Lk 2:4.

6. See Mt 1:15-16.

7. See Lk 2:1-5.

8. Lk 16:7.

9. Lk 16:23.

10. Lk 17:40-51.

11. Lk 18:1.

12. Lk 18:8 ff. and vv. 28-29.

13. 2 Sam 11:2-17.

14. 2 Sam 12:24.

15. Sir 47:2, 11.

16. We could use the meeting between Jacob and Rachel (Gen 29:11, 18), the first nuptial meeting revealed to us in Scripture, to help us discover the unique character of the meeting between Joseph and Mary. See Part II, Ch. 7, p. 135.

17. See Part II, Ch. 4, p. 103.

18. Lk 1:34.

19. The author uses this expression to indicate the love characteristic of friendship, the love between two friends. The expression originally comes from Saint Thomas Aquinas: *amor amicitiae*. See *Summa Theologica*, I-II, q. 26, a. 4; II-II, q. 23, a. 1 [hereinafter "*Summa*"], where Saint Thomas distinguishes the love present in friendship from the love on the level of the concupiscence. [Trans.]

20. Mt 1:19; cf. Acts 10:2, 22.

21. Lk 1:35.

22. Lk 1:38.

23. Judg 13:8.

24. Cf. note 33 below.

25. Mt 1:18-24.

26. Rom 11:29.

27. Mt 3:17, 12:18 (Is 42:1), 17:5; Mk 1:11; Lk 3:22; 2 Pet 1:17.

28. He also conceals her from the devil: this is a theme dear to the Church Fathers. See Part II, Ch. 2, p. 76.

29. Lk 2:4-7.

30. Rev 12:4.

31. Is 7:14.

32. 1 Sam 1:3, 11, etc.

33. Cf. Saint Bernard, *Second Sermon on the Glories of the Virgin Mother* (*Supra Missus Est*), § 9: "Let us turn to the conception and childbirth of the Virgin.... I contemplate there Light without splendor, the Word without speech (*Verbum in-fans*), Water Which is thirsty, and Bread That feels hunger." See *Sermons for the Seasons and Principal Festivals of the Year* (Westminster, Md.: The Carroll Press, 1950), pp. 77-78.

34. Lk 2:16.

35. Lk 2:14.

36. Mt 1:25: "...he knew her not until she had borne a son; and he called His name Jesus" (*Yehoshua*, "The Lord (*Yahweh*) saves"). See note 109.

37. Lk 2:22-24.

38. Lk 2:29-32.

39. Lk 2:33.

40. Scripture does not explicitly state that Simeon was a priest, but Cajetan, the great commentator on Saint Thomas, considers that

since Simeon took it upon himself to bless Mary, Joseph and the Child in the Temple he was undoubtedly a priest (the function of the priest being to bless and to offer sacrifice).

41. Lk 2: 34-35.

42. See Mt 2:1-6; Mic 5:1.

43. Mt 2:11.

44. Lk 1:51-53.

45. Mt 2:13-15.

46. Lk 2:16-18; Jer 31:15.

47. Is 9:5.

48. Lk 1:78.

49. Mt 2:19-23.

50. Lk 2:39-40.

51. Acts 4:32.

52. Lk 2:41.

53. Lk 2:42-47.

54. Cf. Jn 18:37.

55. Lk 2:48.

56. Lk 2:50.

57. Lk 2:51-52.

58. Cf. Jn 2:12: "After this He went down to Capernaum, with His mother and His brethren and His disciples..."

59. Lk 17:10.

60. Sir 47:19.

61. 1 Kings 11:4, 6.

62. 1 Kings 11:43.

63. As a father once said when his only son—the last to bear his name—entered the religious life: "My family name ends in God" ("Mon nom se termine en Dieu").

64. The word "sensible" here means "implying the senses and affections." [Trans.]

65. Cf. 1 Pet 2:5, 9; Rev 1:6, 5:10, 20:6. The Second Vatican Council (see especially *Lumen gentium*, §§ 10–11) insisted strongly upon the importance of the royal priesthood of the faithful, which has its origin in the unique priesthood of Christ, as does the ministerial priesthood. Yet the latter is ordered to the royal, "mystical"

priesthood of the faithful. "The ministerial priest, by the sacred power he enjoys, teaches and rules the priestly people; acting in the person of Christ, he makes present the eucharistic sacrifice, and offers it to God in the name of all the people" (ibid., §10). The faithful, "Taking part in the eucharistic sacrifice…offer the Divine Victim to God, and offer themselves along with it" (ibid., §11). In the same way that the act proper to the priesthood of Christ is the offering of Himself as a victim of love, to glorify the Father and to save us, so too does the royal priesthood, for the faithful (and for the priest), consist in offering one's life for one's brethren, in the footsteps of Jesus and in Him: "Love one another as I have loved you" (Jn 15:12).

66. Acts 6:2.

PART TWO: LIVING WITH SAINT JOSEPH

CHAPTER 1: THE WORKER

67. Mt 1:20.

68. Mt 1:16.

69. Mt 25:21-23, cf. 24:45; Lk 19:17.

70. In *Divini Redemptoris* (1937), his encyclical on atheistic communism issued on March 19, the Feast of Saint Joseph, Pope Pius XI warned of the danger of reducing the notion of poverty to the material poverty of the working classes and of forgetting that there is such a thing as spiritual poverty, which is the first of the Beatitudes (see §§ 44 and 45). At the end of his encyclical, Pius XI wrote: "We place the vast campaign of the Church against world Communism under the standard of Saint Joseph, her mighty Protector. He belongs to the working-class, and he bore the burdens of poverty for himself and the Holy Family, whose tender and vigilant head he was. To him was entrusted the Divine Child when Herod loosed his assassins against Him. In a life of faithful performance of everyday duties, he left an example for all those who must gain their bread by the toil of their hands. He won for himself the title of 'The Just Man,' and thus serves as a living model of that Christian justice which should reign in social life" (ibid., § 81).

70b. "Positivism" refers to the philosophical claim that only what is scientifically verifiable (i.e. measurable) exists.

71. Gal 3:25-28: "But now that faith has come…through faith you are all children of God in Christ Jesus. For all of you who were baptized into Christ have clothed yourselves with Christ. There is neither

Jew nor Greek, there is neither slave nor free man, there is not male nor female; for you are all one in Christ Jesus."

72. It has taken the Church a long time to speak about how a Christian should work. Pope John Paul II's encyclical *Laborem exercens* ("On Human Work") (1981) was an important and very necessary document, because work today has deviated from its true purpose. Why did the Church wait so long to say something about work? The reason is surely because in former days monks were there to set the example; Christians lived close to monks, who were great workers. But work gradually became secularized, such that it has become the means by which mankind has striven to become as autonomous as possible, to such an extent that he is able to declare his independence from God (the myth of Prometheus taken up by Marx: Prometheus stole fire from the gods and thus obtained independence from them).

73. Jn 6:27.

74. Cf. encyclical *Laborem exercens*, § 25, where *Gaudium et spes* is cited: "Man, created in God's image, received a mandate to subject to himself the earth and all that it contains, and to govern the world with justice and holiness; a mandate to relate himself and the totality of things to Him Who was to be acknowledged as the Lord and Creator of all. Thus, by the subjection of all things to Man, the name of God would be wonderful in all the earth."

The constitution *Gaudium et spes* emphasizes strongly here the link between work and adoration.

75. See M.-D. Philippe, *"I Thirst," Conferences on the Wisdom of the Cross*, pp. 63-65.

76. See Part II, Ch. 5.

77. Gen 3:19.

78. Cf. Ex 20:9, 23:12, 34:21; Lev 23:3; Deut 5:13, etc.

79. Cf. Deut 14:29 and 15:9-10. Do we think, sometimes, to ask the Holy Spirit to allow us, through the gift of understanding, to work in the light of Christ, and with Him? It is not about trying to meditate while we work; if we try to we will end up working very poorly... and meditating poorly too! It is about desiring to do everything in the light of Christ, with Him, and for Him, with a great purity of intention—"Blessed are the pure in heart, for they shall see God" (Mt 5:8). We can live by this beatitude (which is the fruit of the gift of understanding) when we work in the presence of God, since the gift of understanding purifies our hearts and leaves

us with only one desire: that of constantly conforming ourselves to the will of the Father for us. Then our work is a witness to our love. Saint Thérèse of the Child Jesus understood this in an astonishing way: what we *do* is secondary; what is important is the *way* in which we do it. Saint Thomas, before her, had already affirmed this as a theologian. Thérèse expresses this in a style of her own, as a little child of God in today's world, but Saint Thomas had said it admirably by showing that there are different ways of doing what we have to do: we can do what we do as a servant, as a friend, or as a child. The servant pays great attention to the result, since the master is unhappy if the job is not well done. The friend is less attentive to the result, his concern being more about *cooperating* with his friend. As for the child, he is not too concerned about the result; he does things well, but does so with love in order to please, in a direct and immediate bond with the person whom he wishes to please. This is what the gift of understanding does: it teaches us to work not for our own glory, nor with a primary concern for the result, but in order to witness to our bond with Christ, so that our own work might be always linked to the great labor of the Cross.

80. Cf. Jn 5:41.

81. See Ch. 5, p. 109.

82. When we waste time, or become a little lazy, the devil immediately infiltrates our psychology. If, on the contrary, we are workers who are greatly devoted to our work, careful not to waste time (because God has given us this time to work) then there is no longer any room for the devil. We must ask for this grace—the grace to understand that we always do our work in the light of God the Creator and in the light of Christ the Redeemer Who comes to accomplish the Father's work by restoring the creature who has been damaged by sin. Everything that comes from the hands of God is great. Sin damaged it all, but Christ gathered everything up again in the mystery of the Cross and through this He gives work a new meaning.

83. It is our imagination and our self-absorption that turns us into dilettantes. Simone Weil says that "dilettantism is detestable, even in art." But it is particularly detestable among religious, since it corrupts the goods that come from God. If we allow ourselves to fall into dilettantism, we are forgetting that we are servants of God. This is why we need to detect it very quickly in our lives. Dilettantism is sometimes well thought of in the world: we give the impression of being easy-going about everything... It makes us look good! But in the religious life it's loathsome: we don't do

anything well, we make no effort to work properly; we don't even ask to learn how something should be done and we make big mistakes, thinking that it doesn't matter because "we have never done it before." But all we have to do is learn! We have to *learn* how to work, be it intellectually or manually; this is very important. We need to acquire a good working ethic so that we do not waste time. There is nothing more irritating for workers, for the poor, for those who know the value of time and cannot stand it when time is wasted, than dilettantism. For dilettantism is just that: we waste time. But if we are Christians then we must understand that the time God gives us is so that, through work, we might be prepared for the Eucharist, through work. It is through work that we dispose ourselves to live on the Eucharist.

84. The Christian faith is wholly turned towards the vision of God: "Now this is eternal life, that they should know You, the only true God, and the one Whom You sent, Jesus Christ" (Jn 17:3). Faith is not given by God simply so that the Christian can live an upright moral life but so that he can "believe in Love" (1 Jn 4:16) and enter, through the adhesion of faith, into the life of the Most Holy Trinity itself: "Believing that a Being called Love dwells in us at every moment of the day and night and that He asks us to live in communion with Him…" Blessed Elizabeth of the Trinity, Letter 330, in *The Complete Works*, Vol. II, "Letters from Carmel" (D.C.: ICS Publications, 1995), p. 354.

　　While we are on earth, contemplation is lived in the nakedness and darkness of faith. But faith is "the substance of things hoped for" (Heb 11:1), which means that the divine reality to which we adhere by faith is already given to us substantially. It is for this reason that Saint Thérèse, despite her great trial of faith, could say at the end of her life, "I really don't see what I'll have after death that I don't already possess in this life. I shall see God, true; but as far as being in His presence, I am totally there here on earth." *The Yellow Notebook*, May 15, in *Her Last Conversations*, trans. John Clarke, O.C.D. (D.C.: ICS Publications, 1977), p. 45.

85. This conference was given to the Novices of the Community of Saint John.

86. It is not always easy to perceive the will of the Father through the work that we have to do. In religious life it is easy, because we live under obedience, but in the world it is much more difficult. When we freely choose a job, or what we are going to do in life, how can we know whether it is the will of God? When you are a religious you have made a free choice of the religious life, but you do not

choose the work that you do. You do not enter religious life to be a stonemason all your life, nor indeed to be a philosopher or a theologian all your life. You enter the religious life to give yourself fully, and to accomplish the will of the Father, which will become concrete in one way or another. Saint Benedict understood clearly that obedience comes before efficiency in work. But this is quite disconcerting for people nowadays, because today we seek efficiency above all else, and all the criteria for work are criteria of efficiency.

87. Jn 5:17, cf. 9:4.

88. Cf. Jn 17:4, 4:34, 5:36, 9:4, 10:32, 37.

89. It is clear that as the Son of God Jesus had no need to be taught to work with His hands, nor to read the Torah. (According to the Jewish tradition, a child passes from the care of his mother to the care of his father at the age of twelve; his mother has taught him to read the Torah, and, from the age of twelve onwards, his father teaches him a trade.) Thanks to His infused knowledge, Jesus would have known how to do both of these without being taught. Yet He wanted to be schooled by Joseph, as He had been by Mary. He wanted to be "subject to them," "to grow in stature and in wisdom" (cf. Lk 2:51-52).

90. Let us apply this to the theologian: the theologian, in order to be a *true* theologian, must work in spiritual poverty. The glory of the theologian is to be poor in order to let God go first and seize him entirely, as God did with Joseph.

91. Jn 18:37.

92. Cf. Mt 19:6; Mk 10:9.

93. Cf. *Laborem exercens*, § 27: "The Christian finds in human work a small part of the Cross of Christ and accepts it in the same spirit of redemption in which Christ accepted His Cross for us. In work, thanks to the light that penetrates us from the Resurrection of Christ, we always find a glimmer of new life, of the new good, as if it were an announcement of 'the new heavens and the new earth'" (cf. 2 Pet 3:13; Rev 21:1).

94. The mystery of the Finding in the Temple is a trial which anticipates for Joseph the mystery of the Cross. See Ch. 2, p. 73 and Ch. 3, note 179.

95. Cf. *Laborem exercens*: "The Church considers it her task always to call attention to the dignity and rights of those who work..." (§ 1), because she "is convinced that work is a fundamental dimension of man's existence on earth" (§ 4).

96. See *Laborem exercens*, §§ 26 and 27.

97. On the poverty of Joseph, see in particular Ch. 5, p. 110 ff.

CHAPTER 2: SPOUSE OF MARY

98. See Ch. 6, pp. 124-124.

99. He is of course presented as a "son of David" (Mt 1:20), "of the house and lineage of David" (Lk 2:4), but at the end of the genealogy of Christ he is presented in relation to Mary.

100. Mt 1:16.

101. See Ch. 5.

102. Song 4:1.

103. See Ch. 6, p. 120 and note 249.

104. See Ch. 3, pp. 82-83.

105. She could not strictly take a vow of virginity, since she was "subject to the Law" (Gal 4:4) and the Law did not allow anyone to be dispensed from having children (because of the coming of the Messiah): "no man or woman among you shall be childless" (Deut 7:14). Therefore she took a vow of virginity "under the condition that it were pleasing to God" (*Summa*, III, q. 28, a. 4). See M.-D. Philippe, *Mary, Mystery of Mercy* (Stockbridge, Mass.: John Paul II Institute of Divine Mercy, 2002), pp. 61 ff; *The Mystery of Mary*, pp. 51 ff.

Cf. Saint Bernard, *Sermon for the Sunday in the Octave of the Assumption*, § 9, in *Sermons for the Seasons and Principal Festivals of the Year* (Westminster, Md.: The Carroll Press, 1950), pp. 269-70: "That which rendered particularly illustrious both the integrity of her flesh and her vow of virginity was the very novelty of her holy purpose: because namely, in liberty of spirit (cf. 2 Cor 3:17) going beyond all the prescriptions of the Mosaic Law, she consecrated her virginity to God by vow, that she might be spotlessly 'holy in body and in spirit' (1 Cor 7:34). And she proved the immovable firmness of her resolve by the constancy of will implied in her answer to the Angel's promise of a son: 'How shall this be done because I know not man?' (Lk 1:34). Likely enough, the reason why she was at first troubled at the greeting of Gabriel 'and thought within herself what manner of salutation this might be' (v. 29) was the fact that he pronounced her 'blessed among women,' whereas it had ever been her wish to be blessed among virgins. Consequently, on hearing from the Angel the words, 'Blessed art thou among women,' she 'thought within herself what manner of salutation this might be,' for it seemed to her to have a suspicious sound. But the moment the danger to her virginity appeared manifest in the promise of a son, she could no longer conceal her alarm and said, 'How shall this be done, because I know not man?' Deservedly therefore, did she obtain the one blessing without forfeiting the other, so that her virginity derived a great increase of glory from her fruitfulness and her fruitfulness in like manner was enhanced by her virginity: as two stars that seem to borrow additional brightness from each other's rays. For it is doubtless a grand thing to be a virgin; but to be a virgin and a mother at once—that is something far greater and grander in every way."

106. Lk 1:35.

107. See Saint Thomas, *Summa*, I-II, q. 28, a. 2; II-II, q. 29, a. 3; q. 104, a. 3. *Contra Gentiles*, III, Ch. 95 and 151; cf. IV, Ch. 22.

108. Lk 1:28, 38.

109. Mt 1:18. Saint Jerome emphasizes that "it does not follow that they came together afterwards; the Scripture shows that this did not happen." *Commentary on Matthew*, in *Liturgical Readings*, for the Vigil of the Nativity (Saint Meinrad, Ind.: Grail Publications, 1954), p. 15. Saint Jerome is defending Mary's virginity against the Arian Helvidius, who was attacking monastic life and consecrated virginity. To say "before eating a meal in the port at Rome, I set sail for Africa," does not necessarily mean that I ever ate that meal; I had the *intention* of eating it, but my sailing to Africa prevented me from doing so. This example must have amused Saint Thomas, who cites it in his *Commentary on Matthew*, I (Marietti Edition, no. 110) and in the *Summa* (III, q. 28, a. 3, ad 1). In the *Summa*, Saint Thomas also cites another example given by Saint Jerome in his treatise against Helvidius: "'Until' does not necessarily have a determined temporal sense (as in Gal 3:19). When the psalmist says: 'Our eyes are turned to the Lord until He have mercy on us' (Ps 122:2), this does not mean that, once we have obtained mercy from God, we shall take our eyes off Him" (loc. cit., ad 3).

Let us note also the following passage in Saint Ambrose: "...it is not necessary to alter what the Evangelist says: '*He knew her not till she brought forth her* Son'; for that is an idiom of Scripture, as ye see in another place: '*Until ye shall have grown old, I am He.*' Surely, God did not cease to be after their old age? And in the Psalm: '*The Lord said unto my Lord: "Sit Thou at My right hand, until I make Thine enemies the footstool of Thy feet."*' Will He not sit there afterwards too? Indeed, because he who guides the cause thinks it suffices to say that it is the cause, he does not seek the superfluous; it is enough for him to affirm the cause undertaken and defer what befalls. And, therefore, he who had undertaken to prove the incorrupt mystery of the Incarnation thought it fruitless to pursue evidence of Mary's Virginity, lest he be seen as a defender of the Virgin, rather than an advocate of the mystery. Surely, when he taught that Joseph was righteous, he adequately declared that he could not violate the Temple of the Holy Spirit, the Mother of the Lord, the womb of the mystery." *Exposition of the Holy Gospel According to Luke*, 2d ed. (Etna, Calif.: Center for Traditionalist Orthodox Studies, 1998), II, par. 6, p. 44.

110. Mt 19:6; Mk 10:9.

111. Cf. Deut 32:10; Ps 17:8; Zec 2:12.

112. "Prevenient": from the Latin *praevenio*, meaning "to precede." This expression (see *Summa*, I-II, q. 111, a. 3) comes from Psalm 59:11 in the Vulgate: *Deus meus, misericordia ejus praeveniet me*, "My God's mercy shall go before me." Saint Thérèse of the Child Jesus had a very acute sense of the prevenient mercy of God. See the end of *Manuscript C*, in *Story of a Soul*, trans. John Clarke, O.C.D. (D.C.: ICS Publications, 1976), p. 256: "Your love has gone before me ever since my childhood"; and p. 259: "It is not because God, in His anticipating [prevenient] mercy, has preserved my soul from mortal sin...."

113. Even when God unites two people very deeply in fraternal charity—in this case two saints—He still remains first, and thus can always ask for solitude. Solitude is always necessary if we want to progress further. In the mystery of the Annunciation, God takes possession of Mary in a "loving theft," and therefore in solitude. It is not that Joseph is not worthy of being present, but it is so that we understand that love for God always has priority. Love for God and love for one's neighbor are one and the same love but are exercised in two different ways, and an order exists between the two: love for God always comes first, and when it does not come first fraternal charity is corrupted—it is no longer according to the order of God's wisdom.

Seized by God's love in this way, Mary does not mind that she is alone, nor that she must keep silent and is, as it were, separated from Joseph, momentarily and emotionally, for she is seized by and drawn to the Father. It is within this great solitude that she utters her *fiat*, a *fiat* that is so personal and so contemplative, since she "conceives in her heart [or "in her spirit"] before she conceives in her flesh" (see Ch. 6, note 250). She cannot ask anyone for advice; she can only allow herself to be seized by the Holy Spirit Who "comes upon her," and then give herself up to Him entirely.

114. We shall be alone with God in the beatific vision, and our friends will be happy for us to be alone, as we ourselves shall be happy for them to be alone with God, since this is our only beatitude, and the *absolute* beatitude. Our beatitude is not to be with a creature whom we love very much; it is to be alone with God. Here we touch upon the created spirit and what it is—the created spirit which requires this solitude, and which requires being bound directly to God.

In adoration here on earth we are already absolutely alone with God, since, in our inmost depths, there is something that is an absolute secret between Him and us: God creates my unique spiritual soul, and in the act of adoration I recognize my radical dependence upon God-the-Creator Who is my Father. The created spirit is, as such, alone with the One Who creates it, and it is vital for the created spirit to recognize this absolutely free gift of love (which gives it *being*)—hence the importance of adoration. This solitude of the created spirit with its Creator and its Father remains fundamental in the state of beatitude. Fraternal charity will of course still exist in heaven, because, as Saint Thomas says, charity is a "participation in the infinite charity which is the Holy Spirit" (see *Summa*, II-II, q. 24, a. 7; q. 23, a. 3, ad 3). Yet it is not fraternal charity which *constitutes* beatitude; fraternal charity is rather a radiance, a profusion of that beatitude.

It is clear that, on earth, our solitude with God in adoration and our desire for contemplation do not in any way exclude love for one's neighbor, for Jesus came to reveal to us the new commandment which is "like" the first (cf. Mt 22:39): "*As* the Father has loved Me, so have I loved you ... love one another *as* I have loved you" (Jn 15:9, 12). And loving *as* Jesus has loved us, i.e. *as* the Father has loved Him (Jn 15:9), does not mean doing one's best to love one's neighbor by conforming to a model. We can only love our brothers *as* Jesus loves them if we strive to be united to Jesus to the point of becoming one with Him, of no longer living except in Him, as Saint Paul says: "It is no longer I who live, but Christ Who lives in me" (Gal 2:20). Fraternal charity on earth is the first fruit of our unity with the three Divine Persons, and without it there can be no true contemplation. While we are still living in faith, we must never forget that "he who does not love his brother whom he has seen *cannot love* God Whom he has not seen" (1 Jn 4:20). "No man has ever seen God; if we love one another, God abides in us and His love is perfected in us" (4:12). Fraternal charity is a fruit of our life of intimacy with God (the gift of wisdom links the two), and it also disposes us to enter more deeply into intimacy with God.

115. When one loves someone very much one never doubts his fidelity; one cannot: it would be contrary to love to do so. We start to doubt someone's fidelity when our love no longer has the same ardor that it had at the beginning. Someone who loves ardently will never say to the wife he has chosen, "You will not betray me!" To say that would prove that he did not love her. We are faithful because we love: faithfulness is a consequence of love, and every true and profound love demands faithfulness, a faithfulness right to the very end.

116. We shall also quote that beautiful passage in Saint Jerome: "…it is commanded in the Law that not only those guilty, but also those having knowledge of the crime are liable to the punishment of the sin. How can Joseph, since he concealed the crime of his wife, be described as a just man? But this testimony is Mary's—that Joseph, *knowing* her chastity and marveling at what had happened, kept secret the mystery of which he was ignorant… Indeed, in the attitude of one paying respect the angel speaks to Joseph in a dream in order to confirm the justice of his silence" (op. cit., p. 15). Origen also forcefully maintains that Joseph did not doubt Mary: cf. note 117.

117. Cf. Saint Thomas, *Commentary on Matthew*, I, no. 117: "According to Jerome and Origen, Joseph had no suspicion of adultery because he knew the modesty and chastity of Mary. Moreover, he had read in Scripture that the virgin would conceive (7:14) and that 'a shoot shall sprout from the stock of Jesse, and from his roots a bud shall blossom' (11:1). He knew also that Mary was descended from the line of David. Thus it was easier for him to believe that Isaiah's prophecy had been accomplished in her than to think that she could have let herself descend into debauchery. This is why, considering himself unworthy to live with a person of such great sanctity, he wanted to send her away again secretly—like when Peter says to Jesus, 'Depart from me, Lord, for I am a sinful man!' (Lk 5:8)." See also Saint Bernard, *Second Sermon on the Glories of the Virgin Mother* (*Supra Missus Est*), § 13, p. 85-86.

118. Let us be careful not confuse "stepping aside" with "withdrawing." Withdrawing almost inevitably implies a turning-in on oneself: we feel worthless, and that the person we love wants nothing to do with us, and so we turn in on ourselves; or, when it is more a question of achievement or authority, we resign, we give up. When we "step aside," however, not only do we continue to love the person, but we love them *more*: we have a *greater* love for the person to whom we were bound (and in this way we are bound to them in a more profound way, in poverty) and we also love those whom our beloved loves, *as* our beloved loves them—in poverty and silence.

119. See Ch. 5.

120. Mt 1:20. Is it the angel Gabriel, as for Mary at the Annunciation? Saint Thomas, following certain Church Fathers, says that we may think so (see *Commentary on Matthew*, I, no. 120). The angel says to Mary, "Do not be afraid, Mary, for you have found favor with God" (Lk 1:30), and to Joseph, "Do not be afraid to take Mary into your home..." Mary "sees" the angel who greets her; she has a "bodily apparition," experienced by her senses (not by her imagination) and accompanied by an interior enlightening of her intelligence (cf. *Summa*, III, q. 30, a. 3, ad 1). The angel "appears in a dream" to Joseph four times (Mt 1:20; 2:13, 19, 22), which leads Saint Thomas to remark that Joseph "did not have so excellent a vision as the Blessed Virgin," since it is at the level of the senses that human knowledge (conditioned by the senses) has the greatest certainty (loc. cit., ad 2).

121. We can be plunged into a climate of *psychological* sadness (which can happen for all sorts of human reasons) and yet still possess a *divine* joy. When Saint Thomas asks whether one can be joyful and sad at the same time (cf. *Summa*, I-II, q. 35, a. 3 and 4; III, q. 84, a. 9, ad 2), he answers that one can indeed, in two different domains: we can be divinely joyful but humanly sad. This is very important for living the communal life, where we often hurt each other yet should always be joyful—Saint Paul tells us this insistently (Phil 3:1, 4:4; 2 Cor 6:10; 1 Thess 5:16, etc.). The communal life allows fraternal charity—that love which comes from God—to be exercised; joy is the consequence of love (cf. *Summa*, II-II, q. 28, a. 4; III, q. 70, a. 3). Love makes use of difficulties and suffering in order to grow. We cannot stop at suffering; we can only stop at the person we love. When we remain "touchy" and sad, it proves that our love does not meet our friend *in himself*—that our love only goes as far as how he acts towards us and the things that affect *us*. Our love is not strong enough, not true enough and not pure enough. This is a very accurate way of checking whether our love is "divine" (i.e. whether it is a love in charity, truly exercised in dependence upon the Holy Spirit) or whether it remains too human, at the level of our senses only.

122. Cf. apostolic letter, *Salvifici doloris* ("On the Christian Meaning of Human Suffering") (1984), § 26: "as the individual takes up his cross, spiritually uniting himself to the cross of Christ, the salvific meaning of suffering is revealed before him. He does not discover this meaning at his own human level, but at the level of the suffering of Christ. At the same time, however, the salvific meaning

of suffering descends from the level of Christ to man's level and becomes, in a sense, the individual's personal response. It is then that man finds in his suffering interior peace and even spiritual joy." And § 27: "A source of joy is found in the overcoming of the sense of the uselessness of suffering, a feeling that is sometimes very strongly rooted in human suffering." The fruit of the conversion of men such as Francis of Assisi or Ignatius of Loyola "is not only that the individual discovers the salvific meaning of suffering, but above all that he becomes a completely new person" (§ 26).

123. Rom 4:18.

124. See Ch. 7, note 287.

125. See *Summa*, III, q. 27, a. 3, c. and ad 3.

126. Lk 1:42-45.

127. Mt 1:20. The Greek text says *"gunaika"* (cf. Ch. 7, note 271).

128. Lk 2:1.

129. According to Saint Jerome, "Joseph is said to be the son of David so that Mary, too, might be shown to be from the family of David" (op. cit., p. 15; cf. note 117, above). See also Saint Thomas, *Summa*, III, q. 28, a. 1, ad 2 and q. 31, a. 2, ad 1 (citing Saint Jerome and Saint Augustine). In any case, if being of David's line does indeed give Joseph's heart something "royal," Mary, on the other hand, has something within her which is even more royal, and has no need in this respect to be "of David's line": she is immaculate, and hence the fullness of her grace allows her to be, in an eminent way, "the offspring of God" (Acts 17:29). Perhaps this is the reason that Scripture does not say that she is of David's line?

130. Lk 2:29-32.

131. When we share suffering with someone, even if it is shared in total silence and in a certain absence, we are more profoundly united than we would be if we were close to one another, living solely of things as we would like them to be, in joy. Suffering shared together, in one and the same thanksgiving and in unity, deepens our hearts and allows the action of the Holy Spirit to go much further.

132. Jn 8:26; cf. 12:49. Very few of these teachers will receive it, but there will at least be Nicodemus, whom we may well consider as having been in the Temple that day, listening to Jesus.

132b. The mystery of the Compassion refers to Mary's participation in the redemptive action of Jesus. Although our redemption was accomplished above all through the cross, "Christ's whole life is a mystery of redemption" (*Catholic Catechism*, § 517); and Mary's union with her Son "in the work of salvation is made manifest from the time of Christ's virginal conception up to His death" (ibid., § 964 (quoting *Lumen gentium*, § 57)), culminating at the Cross where "she stood, in keeping with the divine plan, enduring with her only begotten Son the intensity of his suffering, associated herself with his sacrifice in her mother's heart, and lovingly consenting to the immolation of this victim which was born of her" (*Lumen gentium*, § 58).

133. There is a striking parallel between Mary's "why" ("Why have You done this to us?"), the "why" with which Jesus replies ("Why were you looking for Me?") and the last "why," spoken from the Cross: "My God, My God, why have You forsaken Me?" (Mt 27:46; Mk 15:34). Likewise between "*Your father* and I have been looking for You" and Jesus' reply: "Did you not know that I must be about *My Father's* affairs?" (Lk 2:49). Luke emphasizes that "they did not understand…" (2:50). The "Your father" is echoed by Jesus' "My Father." Yet Joseph did not think even for a moment that Jesus was correcting Mary's words, which referred to him. Through Jesus' words, he adhered to the person of the Son of God, and Jesus' reply must have plunged him into a great silence—that silence in which the Holy Spirit "in our hearts cries out, 'Abba! Father!'" (Gal 4:6; cf. Rom 8:15-16). John Paul II notes that, in this reply, Jesus "disclosed the mystery of His person to Mary and Joseph in an unexpected, unforeseen way, inviting them to go beyond appearances and unfolding before them new horizons… Mary and Joseph did not perceive the sense of Jesus' answer, nor the way in which He reacted (apparently a rejection) to their parental concern. With this attitude, Jesus intended to reveal the mysterious aspects of His intimacy with the Father, aspects which Mary [and we could add Joseph] intuited, without knowing how to associate them with the trial she was undergoing." General Audience, Jan 15, 1997, in *Theotokos: Woman, Mother, Disciple*, a compilation of John Paul II's Catecheses on Mary (Boston: Pauline, 2000).

134. Col. 3:3.

135. See Ch. 6.

136. See Ch. 6, p. 124.

137. See Ch. 3.

138. *Letter to the Ephesians*, in *Early Christian Fathers*, Cyril C. Richardson, ed. and trans. (N.Y.: MacMillan Company, 1970), p. 113.

139. *Homilies on Luke*, VI, 4 (D.C.: Catholic University of America Press, 1996), pp. 24-25.

140. *Exposition of the Holy Gospel According to Luke*, II, 3, p. 42.

141. Mt 4:1.

142. Is 62:6. Saint John Damascene also comments on this subject. He says that Mary was entrusted by the priests "to a suitor who was to be, properly speaking, the guardian of her virginity: Joseph… who until his old age had kept the law without compromise, far better than his peers. This holy and spotless maiden now lived with him, remaining at home and knowing nothing of what transpired outside her doors." *On the Dormition of the Holy Mother of God*, Homily I, in *On the Dormition of Mary: Early Patristic Homilies*, trans. Brian E. Daley, S.J. (Crestwood, N.Y.: Saint Vladimir's Seminary Press, 1998), par. 6, p. 190.

CHAPTER 3: THE SERVICE OF AUTHORITY

143. See p. 151.

144. Jn 13:16 and 15:20. Cf. Mt 10:24; Lk 6:40.

145. Phil 2:7.

146. Cf. Eph 3:15.

147. Ex 20:3, 5.

148. Deut 6:5.

149. Lev 19:18.

150. See Jer 7:13 & 25; 11:7, 25:3-4, 26:5, 29:19, 32:33, 35:14-15, 44:4.

151. Acts 7:35. Cf. 1 Sam 12:6.

152. Num 12:7; Josh 1:1-2, 7, etc.

153. See Ex 33:12-17; Num 12:6-8; Sir 45:4, etc.

154. 1 Sam 8:5, 12:12.

155. Gen 15:6; Rom 4:3-22.

156. Cf. Rom 4:16; Gal 3:7-9; Jas 2:21, etc.

157. Sir 3:2.

158. See Ch. 2, p. 59.

159. Those given in the apocryphal *Protoevangelium of James* do not help us very much. See René Laurentin, *A Short Treatise on The Virgin Mary*, trans. Charles Neumann, S.M. (Washington, N.J.: AMI Press, 1991), pp. 81-82.

160. See M.-D. Philippe, *Mary, Mystery of Mercy*, pp. 103 ff.

161. Lk 1:36.

162. Mt 10:16.

163. The two great foundations of the Church, Joseph and Peter (Peter is the "column" [cf. Ch. 7, note 298], but it is also *upon him* that Jesus builds His Church: cf. Mt 16:18), both find themselves, from

the very first moment of their prudent leaderships, confronted by things which they do not understand. Peter asks Jesus, "And him [John], what is to become of him?" and Jesus replies, "Don't worry about him. If I want him to stay, what does it matter to you?" Peter cannot understand. When someone becomes a leader, he likes to see things clearly. But the first thing that Jesus requires of Peter is to accept not to understand, and what's more, not to understand something about the person whom Jesus loves the most! If it had been something about Thomas, or Philip, or Jude, that would have been easier. But it is John, he whom Jesus loves so much.

Joseph, the patriarch of patriarchs, is also a man of government, faithful and prudent. He starts to shoulder the greatest responsibility of all: being the guardian of Mary, in love. He chose Mary, and Mary chose him, and he is responsible for her before men and before God. And the first thing that he perceives is that Mary is expecting a child and has said nothing to him about it. This is even more difficult to accept than what Peter had to accept.

It is interesting to see that the prudence of the Christian who has a position of responsibility in the Church (prudence transformed by faith, under the action of the gift of counsel), finds himself confronted first of all by something that is incomprehensible. Accepting something which is beyond his understanding is the most difficult thing to do for someone who has to lead or govern. Peter could have said, "If it is like that, then I cannot feed Christ's sheep, because I don't know what will happen to the sheep *par excellence*—John; for 'the good shepherd knows his sheep and his sheep know him'" (cf. Jn 10:14).

Joseph the patriarch also faces this trial, and we must look at the way in which the Holy Spirit works upon his heart. The Holy Spirit, the "Father of the poor," always chooses His moment well. It is when Joseph is betrothed to Mary—thus during the fervor of his "first love"—that the Holy Spirit hollows out in him a spirit of poverty in his government over her for whom he is responsible. He must accept not to understand. This is a great trial, but a divine trial, and thus has a positive purpose. When God tests us it is never something negative: it is always so that we go further in loving. This is what is so wonderful about divine government. When we put each other to the test, it can be negative; when God tests us, it is never negative.

164. See Ch. 4, p. 95.

165. Obviously, if we do not believe in angels then we cannot understand any of this. Here we touch very precisely upon the contradictions of the devil: in an age when humanity insists on freedom, it rejects the existence of angels. In an age when theologians focus

only upon freedom, they reject the angels, forgetting that the angels are our elder brothers who allow us to live in a greater freedom. Thanks to His intermediaries, God leaves us our freedom. We can see it here in Joseph's case, just as we saw it for Mary.

166. Up to this point, Joseph had been bound to Mary for her own sake. From this point onwards a new bond exists, a bond with Mary carrying within her the Son of God, Who is *her* Son. There is something completely new in Mary: the mystery of her divine motherhood. Joseph did not choose the Mother of God; he could not have done so. He could only choose Mary, consecrated to God. A new grace was therefore needed so that he could see Mary as the Mother of God.

167. This is only to be expected: an angel does not talk for the sake of talking, for his mission is accomplished within his contemplation.

168. Cf. Jn 1:29-30.

169. Jn 19:27. Cf. Ch. 7, p. 127 ff.

170. Lk 2:3-5.

171. Ibid. 2:6.

172. Mt 22:21; Mk 12:17; Lk 20:25.

173. Ambrose, *Exposition of the Holy Gospel According to Luke*, II:44, p. 62.

174. Mt 2:11.

175. See Ch. 7, p. 135.

176. Since the Church likes to apply the words concerning Wisdom to Mary, we could undoubtedly also apply to her the following verses from Job: "She is hidden from the eyes of all the living, and concealed from the birds of the air.... God understands the way to her, and He knows her place" (28:21, 23).

177. Lk 2:16.

178. Mt 11:25; Lk 10:21.

179. For the first time since Jesus' birth, Joseph and Mary find themselves alone together. They do not blame each other, as we would have done in our human way: "You should have warned me! You could have told me! I thought he was with you," etc. We can imagine what the conversation would have been like in an ordinary family. Here, however, there is a great silence of love. Yet worry and suffering still grip their hearts because they do not understand this attitude on the part of the child Jesus, indeed they cannot understand it. Had Jesus warned them, had He said to them, "Please agree that I stay with the teachers of the Law for a few days, and please stay with Me during that time," they would have readily

agreed, and done so with a lot of love. But He has not said anything. This is always the hardest thing to endure when one is suffering: not being able to understand the meaning of the suffering. And
it is particularly hard for a man's heart to endure, because a man
always wants to see things clearly; a man likes to understand what
is going on. So there was a very far-reaching purification in Joseph's
heart, a purification which bound him closely to Mary's heart, for it
is in a suffering lived together that two people who love each other
are drawn most closely together.

Together they go back to Jerusalem and look for Jesus. And
when they find Him again, it is not Joseph who speaks to Him but
Mary. And yet Joseph is the one who has authority! However, he
remains quiet and says nothing. It is Mary who questions Jesus,
"Why have You done this to us? Behold, *Your father* and I have
been looking for You…" And Joseph, who had been entrusted with
the safekeeping of the child, hears Jesus reply, "Why were you
looking for Me?"—when it was perfectly natural that they should
have been looking for Him! The Cross is always something that
our intelligence cannot grasp, something that escapes our understanding. Had Jesus had given them an explanation, had He
apologized, Joseph and Mary would have said, "Let's not speak
about it anymore; it's all right, we understand." But Jesus does not
apologize. He wants to draw Joseph and Mary towards the Father:
"Did you not know that I must be about My Father's affairs?" He
wants to draw them to where He Himself dwells: "Do you not
believe that I am in the Father? …Believe Me: I am in the Father
and the Father is in Me" (Jn 14:10, 11). Cf. Ch. 2, note 133.

180. Lk 2:51. Origen, commenting this verse, emphasizes that Joseph
made no mistake about the submission of the Child-God, and says
that "it was in trembling that he gave his orders."

CHAPTER 4: MAN OF PRUDENCE

181. We use the term "passion" here in the sense in which Saint Thomas
uses it. See *Summa*, I-II, qq. 22-30. The passional impulse may either
be simply the fruit of the attraction of a sensible good (this is what
we call the domain of the "concupiscible"), or the fruit of the attraction of a sensible good that is difficult to acquire, in which case there
exists a struggle (this is the domain of the "irascible"). See M.-D.
Philippe, *Retracing Reality*, pp. 69 ff.

182. These so-called "cardinal" virtues constitute the great human heritage.
When we destroy them, we destroy the very foundation of the human
person. The acquisition of virtues is thus something very important.

We should not be too ready today to speak about education being ordered toward the virtues, because that frightens people away; but we need to know it. We may use other terms, such as "values" (this is one way of talking about it without frightening people away), but the word "virtue" is misunderstood; it has lost its original sense, which had nothing off-putting about it: *aretè* in Greek designates a capacity to operate in a way that is just, true and profound. It would be good to find a new word to express this properly.

183. Cf. Jn 14:31; Phil 2:8; Rom 5:19; Heb. 5:8.

184. On the three levels of ethics—the fundamental human level, the religious level and the Christian level—see M.-D. Philippe, "Quelques réflexions pour une philosophie éthique" in *Aletheia*, nos. 1-2 (Nov 1992), pp. 20 ff.

185. Cf. Mt 13:33; Lk 13:20-21.

186. Jn 17:3.

187. Cf. Ch. 1, note 84. Faith is not necessary in order to know what man is, i.e. in order to develop a philosophy. This is where we need to correct the laziness we may have in claiming that faith is all we need. Faith presupposes that our intelligence will seek to reach all that it can reach by itself. This is much more powerful and much truer. There is something very important and noble in the respect that grace has for nature. Jesus did not suppress the first Adam, even though He Himself could have been the Adam of a new humanity. He did not change the Creator's vision of mankind; He did not change human nature. We hold our human nature from our first father, from our first parents—Adam and Eve—and, as a consequence of the first sin, our human nature knows an unbalance that will last our whole lives long.

188. Knowing that we are made for the beatific vision, and that the beatific vision takes place, according to the Book of Revelation (19:7-9; 21:2 ff.), in the nuptial union of our souls with Jesus, one chooses the contemplative religious life in order to respond to this loving choice Christ makes of us, and one thereby directs everything towards the beatific vision. Saint Thomas says that the contemplative life is an anticipation of the beatific vision (*Summa*, II-II, q. 180, a. 4). For every Christian, silent prayer is this anticipation, through the betrothal of his soul to Jesus, through the choice of love made between his soul and Jesus. Jesus leads us towards the Father; He has us live His own "return to the Father," His *Vado ad Patrem* (Jn 14:12, 28; 16:17, 28; 17:11, 13; 20:17), and the Father "prunes" us (Jn 15:2 ff.) to this end.

189. See *Commentary on Saint John*, II, nos. 338 to 343.

190. 1 Jn 4:19; cf. 4:10.

191. Mk 10:21. At the natural level, within the order of our radical dependence upon the Creator, we already live on God's gaze which gives us being. "I love you for yourself": the Creator says this to us at every moment. At every moment, through adoration and through our thirst for contemplation, we meet this gaze of the Father upon us: "I love you for yourself." It removes all the uneasiness we may have about who we are, when we know that God loves us for ourselves... And His love for us is *His very self*, giving Himself entirely and loving us entirely. He loves us for ourselves, since He loves us freely and with an infinite capacity for love. And He awaits a gesture of gratitude from us: an act of adoration, by which we recognize that He is our Creator and that He has done everything for us.

192. We are able to contemplate God because we know that He is gazing upon us. It is a contemplation in extreme poverty, a contemplation in receptivity: since God is gazing upon us, we desire to receive and welcome His gaze, and receiving God's gaze means receiving God; it means receiving His love.

193. It is, however, impossible for us to think that Joseph did not choose Mary. Like all the great saints, Joseph and Mary surpassed the conditioning of their era. If we try to understand them and to discover the secret of their hearts looking only at the age in which they lived, then we condemn ourselves to understanding nothing at all.

194. We deliberately say "*a* summit" and not "*the* summit," in the sense that it extends as far as the gift of the body and implies an intense and lasting communal life. It is in this double sense that, in the *Contra Gentiles* (IV, Ch. 123), Saint Thomas speaks of marriage as "the greatest friendship," *maxima amicitia*.

195. *Summa*, III, q. 29, a. 2.

196. See Ch. 5, p. 116.

197. This is why the liturgical feast of the Betrothal of Mary and Joseph (formerly celebrated on January 23) was a very beautiful tradition.

198. "I will give you a new heart and place a new spirit within you, taking from your bodies your hearts of stone and giving you hearts of flesh. I will put My spirit within you" (Ezek 36:26-27; cf. 11:19).

199. Cf. Gen 12:13.

200. Rev 14:4.

201. Cf. Is 54:5, 62:3-5; Hos 2:19-20, 3:1, etc.

202. The gift of counsel sometimes makes us perform acts which go beyond human prudence, but the virtue of prudence still remains, and we must not go beyond it without being sure (as far as possible) that it is indeed the Holy Spirit asking us to. The Holy Spirit *normally* asks us to live as prudent people, but sometimes He asks us—and enables us—to perform heroic acts that go beyond "normal" prudence.

203. See Ch. 5, p. 111.

204. *"La petite balle du Bon Dieu"* see *Manuscript A*, op. cit., pp. 136 and 142; Letters 34, 36, 74, 76, 79.

CHAPTER 5: THE "JUST, GOD-FEARING" MAN

205. Mt 1:19. We discover his other qualities through his actions, in particular his obedience.

206. Ezek 18:5.

207. Ps 15:2.

208. Cf. Prov 20:7.

209. Prov 24:16.

210. See Ps 27:3, 22:5-6, 44:7-9; 2 Mac 8:18, etc.

211. Sir 2:1-8.

212. Sir 32:24 to 33:1.

213. Rom 4; Gal 3:6-7. The author of the Letter to the Hebrews, in recalling that the just, i.e. those who "do the will of God," "shall benefit from the promise," emphasizes the link between faith and eschatological hope (hope in the return of Christ): "For, yet a little while, and the coming one shall come and not tarry; but My righteous one shall live by faith, and if he shrinks back, My soul has no pleasure in him" (10:37-38).

214. Hab 2:4.

215. See (amongst others) Ps 103, 112, 115... Job is indeed a great example of the just man of the Old Testament. The Lord pays him this tribute: "Have you considered My servant Job, and that there is none like him on the earth, a blameless and upright man, who fears God and turns away from evil?" (Job 1:8; cf. 2:3).

216. Ps 111:10; Prov 1:7, 9:10, 15:33; Sir 1:14, 20.

217. Sir 1:16, 18.

218. In the Acts of the Apostles, of the centurion Cornelius (10:22), who is also described as "pious and God-fearing" (10:2).

219. We know that Saint Thomas (following Saint Augustine in his *Explanation of the Sermon on the Mount*), associates the beatitude of "those who are poor in spirit" (Mt 5:3) with the gift of fear. See *Summa*, II-II, q. 19, a. 12.

220. Mt 4:10; Lk 4:8.

221. Deut 6:13.

222. Ps 116:12. See Ch. 4, note 191.

223. Jn 4:23-24.

224. Following, once again, Saint Augustine, Saint Thomas distinguishes "servile" or "worldly" fear from fear that is "filial" or "chaste." See Saint Augustine, *Homilies on the First Epistle of John*, IX, 4-8, in *Nicene and Post-Nicene Fathers*, Vol. 1, First Series, ed. Philip Schaff, 2d ed. (Peabody, Mass.: Hendrickson Publishers, 1995), pp. 515-17; *The City of God*, XIV, 9 (N.Y.: The Modern Library, 1950), p. 455.

    We cannot summarize here the very fine analysis Saint Thomas makes (II-II, q. 19, a. 2 to 9). Let us note only that chaste, filial fear, has two actions: that of revering God and fearing being separated from Him (see I-II, q. 67, q. 4, ad 2), and also that, as love grows, so too does filial fear grow and servile fear disappear (II-II, q. 19, a. 10).

225. Mt 19:18; Mk 10:19; Lk 18:20.

226. See Ps 112.

227. Since it is a question of being perfect "as your heavenly Father is perfect" (Mt 5:48), this perfection of love can be nothing other than a gift of God at work in us, but it is a gift to which we dispose ourselves by living the spirit of the evangelical counsels (cf. the decree *Perfectae caritatis* of the Second Vatican Council, §1). We use the word spirit advisedly here, for striving towards perfect charity, striving to "love to the end" like Christ (Jn 13:1), is not something reserved for religious. It is not only religious whom Christ "makes perfect" by uniting them to the offering that He makes of Himself to the Father. Saint Paul says to all Christians, "For this is the will of God, your sanctification" (1 Thess 4:3). Every Christian who so desires can let himself be attracted by Christ, who "by a single offering...has perfected for all time those who are sanctified" (Heb. 10:14). The most perfect act we can perform on earth is to offer our whole life, everything that we are, in an act of adoration and a thirst for contemplation; thereby we join Jesus as He offers Himself to the Father.

228. Mt 19:21.

229. Mt 22:39.

230. It is from the love that we have for the human person that we discover his rights. In order to respect someone it is necessary to love
him a great deal, and respect consists precisely in recognizing that
he is other than me, and therefore that he has a fundamental right
to exist. This is the most fundamental right: to respect the other
person in what he is and to recognize, in his otherness with respect
to me, that I am not the only one in the world. We have an instinctive propensity to think of ourselves as being the center of the uni-
verse and that everything must be relative to us. Egocentricity
makes it difficult for us to think of the other as other; we think of
him only in relation to ourselves, and hence we become the measure
of others.

The act of justice is thus an act which requires a great lucidity
concerning the fundamental right of the other to exist as a person,
as an individual, in his uniqueness, in his otherness, in his fragility
and also in his power. I must respect someone who appears to me
to be extremely fragile just as much as I respect someone who
appears to have the power to destroy me. This is not respect for
authority; it is respect for the person, respect for the other as other,
and we only discover the other's person by loving him or her. The
recognition of his otherness, with his right to exist, presupposes a
certain love, namely, that love for all people that we call philan-
thropy. There is a natural appetite in us to love man as man, that is
to say, as having this fundamental right to be respected. This is
very important because we very easily tend to respect only those
who have power or who threaten to dominate us. That sort of
respect is not the respect due to the human person.

231. Jn 15:13.

232. Ps 33:20-22. Filial fear (the gift of fear) is closely linked to hope.
Only those who are truly poor have great desires and know that
they must receive everything from God.

233. Since he was a "just man," Joseph also was awaiting the coming of
the Messiah. What Saint Luke says of the elderly Simeon is also
true of Joseph: "...this man was righteous and devout, looking for
the consolation of Israel, and the Holy Spirit was upon him" (Lk
2:25). Joseph was awaiting the Messiah just as Christians await—
or should await—the return of Christ. The Eucharistic liturgy
reminds us of it: "Christ will come again," "Lord Jesus, come in
glory," "...until You come in glory." This is why Joseph should
teach us to await the return of Christ. It is part of the hope of the

poor, and it demands a very radical purification of the heart. It requires us to offer to God all the bonds of love that He has given us so as to desire only one thing: His gracious will for us.

234. In fact, Joseph's magnanimity, his greatness of soul, has something royal about it (there is a close link between true humility and magnanimity). In this he is truly a "son of David," the king of whom the prophet Samuel said, "The Lord has sought out a man after His own heart" (1 Sam 13:14)—which is echoed by Psalm 89:20: "I have found David, My servant...." As Bossuet says, "The time had come for God to seek out a man after His own heart, in order to place into his hands what was most precious to Him—I mean the person of His only Son, the integrity of His holy Mother, the salvation of the human race, the most sacred secret of His counsel, the treasure of heaven and earth" (*Premier panégyrique de saint Joseph*).

235. Let us clarify a little further the distinction between humility and the *spirit of poverty*. Humility is a virtue which we acquire, whereas the spirit of poverty (not to be confused with those poverties that we receive or inherit etc.) is the fruit of a gift of the Holy Spirit, namely the gift of fear. And the gift of fear, in the order of exercise, goes further than humility exercised in a human way.

Humility helps the spirit of poverty, but the spirit of poverty is born from love and enables all the "lacks" that we have to become something positive that unite us to the Cross of Christ. That is why the spirit of poverty goes further than humility, but once again, it requires the acquisition of the virtue of humility. As long as we have not yet acquired humility, pride will keep rearing its head, because (as a consequence of original sin) we are naturally inclined towards pride. There is nothing original about being proud, but being humble is very original! Humility is a rare thing, whereas pride is the most common fault of all.

In order for us to understand better poverty and humility, we should look at their opposites: the spirit of possession and the spirit of pride. There is a beatitude of the poor but there is not a beatitude of the humble, which shows us that poverty is more immediately linked to love. Humility also is linked to love, but it is there to eliminate the obstacles that keep us from loving, for pride is the major obstacle to loving. Someone who is proud always wants to be first, and so he does not accept that, in love, one becomes relative to the other person.

236. Jn 12:8.

237. Mt 7:13; Lk 13:24. Cf. Mt 19:24 (Mk 10:25; Lk 18:25): "It is easier

for a camel to go through the eye of a needle than for a rich man to enter the kingdom of God."

238. The "just" man recognizes that God's rights come first (cf. Ch. 2, p. 65). Although Joseph loves his wife as no other husband will ever love his wife, he understands that his love for Mary gives him no claim over her. On the other hand, when *we* love someone, we very easily think that we have a claim on him: "He is my friend, I can ask anything of him"—and we possess, we want to make him our very own. Joseph never possessed Mary. He understood that the fewer rights he had over her (in other words, the greater his interior poverty), then the more divine love would be able to take possession of everything; and he knew that divine love is never a rival to human love, and that, far from destroying it, divine love allows human love to meet all of its demands. Surely this is Joseph's great secret?

239. God will then give us His light. It is at the very moment when Joseph is plunged into an abyss of poverty (and into a great solitude also, since seeking advice from anyone would have meant betraying Mary) that the angel comes to enlighten him. God only enlightens those who are poor: we have to descend into very deep levels of poverty for God to come and enlighten us directly. As long as we believe that we can get by on our own, He does not come. And we are always a bit like that. We say, "I'll manage to get by, I'm already making progress, things are already better than last year...." But from time to time God knocks us over to help us see that the little progress we have made is not that brilliant! And then we enter into poverty—a poverty that goes very far, and it is at that moment that God enlightens us. We will not necessarily have a visit from an angel during the night like Saint Joseph! But, in faith, we will not have any less either.

240. See Ch. 7, pp. 132-134.

241. 1 Jn 3:18. Saint John uses here the word *ergon* (work) which appears frequently in his Gospel, and with great emphasis, for it is ultimately about working with the Father, cooperating with the work of the Father.

242. See *Summa*, II-II, q. 152, a. 2, ad 5. Saint Thomas is evidently referring to Paul, in particular to 1 Cor 7:32-38.

243. See 1 Kings 18:38.

244. In Saint Joseph, the movement from "servile" fear to "filial" fear, such as Saint Paul expresses it in the Letter to the Romans, is

accomplished in an eminent way: "For all who are led by the Spirit of God are sons of God. For you did not receive the spirit of slavery to fall back into fear, but you have received the spirit of filial adoption, by which we cry, 'Abba! Father!'" (8:14-15). Cf. *Summa*, II-II, q. 19, a. 2.

CHAPTER 6: MAN OF SILENCE, PATRIARCH OF MONASTIC LIFE

245. See Ch. 2, pp. 61-63; Ch. 3, pp. 84-88.

246. See Ch. 2, p. 61.

247. Saint Thomas says, "This is the proper mark of friendship: that one reveal his secrets to his friend. For since charity unites affections and makes, as it were, one heart of two, one seems not to have dismissed from his heart that which he reveals to a friend" (*Contra Gentiles*, IV, Ch. 21; cf. *Commentary on John*, XV, no. 2016).

248. We only tell a secret to someone whom we are sure will not divulge it, whom we are sure will not betray us. There are some people to whom we cannot say anything because everybody else immediately knows what we have said to them! We cannot trust them, therefore. And when someone has once betrayed a secret, we say, "I see; I shall keep silent in the future." But thanks to the Holy Spirit, we can always re-discover a new trust in someone again; if He can restore the dead to life, He can restore a broken trust.

249. Cf. Saint Thomas, *Summa*, I, q. 37, a. 1: "Love is the bond, the knot (*nexus*) of those who love each other; in this way the Holy Spirit is said to be the nexus of the Father and the Son." Cf. *Commentary on John*, XVII, no. 2187: "The Holy Spirit, Who is the nexus of the two." See also VII, no. 1156; II, no. 357.

250. "Blessed is she who believed..." cries Elizabeth (Lk 1:45). "Blessed are those who believe..." says Jesus (Jn 20:29). And to those who proclaim blessed she who carried Christ in her womb, He replies, "Blessed rather are those who hear the word of God and keep it!" (Lk 11:28; cf. 8:21). Saint Augustine comments, "Mary is more blessed in receiving the faith of Christ, than in conceiving the flesh of Christ... Her nearness as a Mother would have been of no profit to Mary, had she not borne Christ in her heart after a more blessed manner than in her flesh" (*Of Holy Virginity*, III, 3; NAPNF, Vol. 3, p. 418). This *Prius concipit in corde* [or *in mente*] *quam in carne* (she "conceived within her heart [or within her spirit] before she conceived within her flesh") is a very strong affirmation, dear to Saint Augustine and which we also find in Saint Leo the Great. Evoked in *Lumen gentium* (§ 53), John Paul II refers to it several

times in his encyclical *Redemptoris Mater* (1987), § 13, where he speaks about it with great clarity.

251. Cf. Ch. 4, p. 106 and Ch. 7, pp. 139-140.

252. When the liturgy of the midnight Mass at Christmas quotes *Filius meus es tu, ego hodie genui te*, "You are my son; today I have begotten you" (Ps 2:7), they are the words of the Father, but this is also what Mary lives...

253. If Mary's motherhood is first of all a contemplative one (as Saint Augustine says), then Joseph is able to enter into this mystery of unity with the Father, and so also, following him, all those who live in a spirit of virginity and who "seek among all the love of only one"—the love of Christ. Saint Augustine continues, saying of such that, despite the fact that they cannot conceive Christ in the womb as Mary did, they nevertheless conceive Him in their hearts (see op. cit., XII, 11).

254. The true man of poverty is always joyful. Why? Because God only impoverishes him so as to be able then to overwhelm his heart. The love of God can only possess His creature if that creature accepts to be possessed by God and *accepts* it even to the point of becoming nothing, of becoming simply a beggar of love and mercy.

255. 1 Tim. 2:5.

256. Heb. 9:15 and 12:24. Cf. 8:6.

257. See *Summa*, I, q. 22, a. 3. Cf. q. 103, a. 6 and *Contra Gentiles*, III, Ch. 77.

258. Mt 5:3.

259. Marthe Robin (1902-1981) was a Catholic Frenchwoman who fell ill in her youth and was bedridden for over 50 years; she received the stigmata at the age of 27, as well as many other mystical graces. She was the founder, along with Fr. Georges Finet, of the Homes of Charity. Her spirituality and writings influenced several French theologians. In 1998, diocesan authorities forwarded her Cause for Beatification to the Vatican.

260. Bossuet says, "This man after the heart of God does not show himself to the outside world" and also, "it is the hidden virtues [those "in which the public takes no part, in which everything takes place between man and God"] which make him worthy of praise... Thus the Christian life should be a hidden life, and the true Christian should ardently desire to dwell in the shadow of God's wings [cf. Ps 17:8; 57:1; 61:4; 63:7 etc.] with no other spectator" (*Premier panégyrique de saint Joseph*).

261. One might be tempted to say that Saint Joseph cannot be the model of fatherhood as regards the family, that he is more a model as regards monastic life—that he is more a monk in the world than a true father of a family with all the difficulties and responsibilities that come with flesh-and-blood fatherhood. But that would be to look at Joseph and at the role of a Christian husband and father in a way that is too exterior.

262. Num 12:8.

263. See Ex 33:18-23.

264. Sir 45:4. Cf. Num 12:7: "Not so with My servant Moses; he is entrusted with all My house."

265. Num 12:3.

266. Adoration puts us in the truth; if we do not adore, we gradually become less capable of seeking the truth.

267. Jn 17:3.

CHAPTER 7: SAINT JOSEPH AND SAINT JOHN

268. John does not speak of Joseph in his Gospel. This is curious, is it not? Mary must often have spoken to him about Joseph, but perhaps she asked John not to speak about him? Perhaps this was a secret that Mary told John for his formation, for we cannot be fully formed in the Christian life without Joseph. On Mary's silence concerning Joseph, let us note that the only explicit mention made of Joseph by Mary is the one she makes when addressing Jesus at the time of the Finding in the Temple—a painful question which she expresses on behalf of Joseph: "Behold, Your father and I..." (Lk 2:48).

269. Jn 19:27.

270. Is 53:3.

271. Rev 21:9; cf. 19:7. In these two passages, Saint John uses the term by which Jesus Himself addresses Mary at Cana (Jn 2:4) and from the Cross (Jn 19:26): *gunai*. At Rev 22:17, however, he says "bride," *nymphè*.

272. Lam 1:12.

273. Cf. Jn 2:1-2: "...the mother of Jesus was there. Jesus also was invited to the marriage, with His disciples."

274. Lk 2:35. Cf. note 132b regarding the "mystery of Compassion."

275. Jn 19:26-27.

276. Saint Thomas asks which of Peter and John Jesus loved more. See *Commentary on John*, XXI, nos. 2635 to 2643 (cf. XIII, no. 1804

and *Summa*, I, q. 20, a. 4). The question allowed him to clarify what is properly characteristic of each of these two bonds of love. Regarding the three qualities of Saint John which Saint Thomas highlights (the perspicacity of his intelligence, his virginity [of body and heart] and his youth: see loc. cit.), let us recall that the tradition of the Fathers and the theologians of the Middle Ages also affirm the virginity of Saint Joseph (see especially Cajetan's *Commentary on the Summa Theologica*, III, q. 28, a. 4).

277. To Mary, *standing* at the foot of the cross as Saint John emphasizes (19:25), we can apply what Ezekiel says (2:2 and 3:24): "The Spirit entered into me and set me upon my feet."

278. 2 Mac 7:20.

279. Cf. Col 1:24.

280. Jn 12:32.

281. The theologian, to be very precise, will say "quasi-infinite," since we distinguish Christ's divine will and His human will (cf. *Summa*, III, q. 18, a. 1).

282. Cf. Saint Thomas, *Compendium Theologiae*, Ch. 216, no. 435: "It was fitting for Christ, author of man's salvation, to possess from the first moment of His Incarnation the full vision of God, and not to arrive at it over time, as other holy men arrive at it." Cf. *Summa*, III, q. 15, a. 10. We are aware that this affirmation is strongly contested today by some theologians, but it comes under the doctrine of the Church, which has not changed.

283. See *Summa*, III, q. 46, a. 8; *Compendium*, Ch. 231 and 232.

284. See *Summa*, I, q. 79, a. 9; Saint Augustine, *The Trinity*, XII, Ch. 1, pars. 2, 3; Ch. 4, par. 22 (Brooklyn, N.Y.: New City Press, 1991), pp. 322-24, 334.

285. Lk 1:45.

286. Jn 19:23; Mt 27:35; Mk. 15:24; Lk 23:34.

287. Mary's Immaculate Conception is an anticipated fruit of the Redemption, as the Papal Bull which proclaims the Immaculate Conception (*Ineffabilis Deus*) states: The most Blessed Virgin Mary... was, by a special grace and privilege of God, in view of the merits of Jesus Christ, her Son and the Redeemer of the human race, preserved free from all stain of original sin." See M.-D. Philippe, "The Immaculate Conception: Masterpiece of the Holy Spirit Through the Cross of Christ" in *The Morning Star*, pp. 243 ff.

288. We see this clearly in the religious life: communal life allows bonds of fraternal charity to be formed with brothers whom we would

never have met elsewhere, or indeed whom we would never have chosen as friends.

289. Jn. 13:34.

290. Cf. Ch. 3, pp. 82-83.

291. Concerning the meaning of the verb "to know" in Mt 1:25 ("and he knew her not until she had borne a son"), Saint Thomas notes that this term does not necessarily have here the carnal sense that it has elsewhere in the Bible, notably in Mary's reply to the angel Gabriel ("I do not know man"). Saint Thomas cites first of all Saint John Chrysostom, who sees this phrase as meaning that, until Jesus was born, Joseph could not yet perceive Mary's full dignity and beauty. He adds that it could also be a question here of knowing by seeing: just as "the Israelites could not look at Moses' face" when he came down from Sinai, "because of its brightness" (2 Cor 3:7), in the same way Mary, "as long as the glory of the power of the Most High covered her with His shadow, could not be known by Joseph. But after the birth she was known by Joseph by the sight of her face, not by carnal relations" (*Summa*, III, q. 28, a. 3, ad 3). To Mary, of whom it is said "the king will desire [her] beauty" (Ps 45:11), is applied that which is said of the king himself: "you are the fairest of the sons of men; grace is poured upon your lips" (Ps 45:2). The bodily beauty of Christ, says Saint Thomas, could not come from being, for example, either blond or redheaded; the bodily beauty which was fitting to His status, and which He possessed totally, was manifest by the radiance upon His face of "something divine" which "made Him revered by all" (*Commentary* on Ps 45:2). We can say that there is something analogous in her of whom it is said "the king desires her beauty." But let us stress "analogous" (i.e. different, but with an element in common) for she is not God, and also because God kept her hidden, as Psalm 45 again says: "All glorious is the daughter of the king within" (v. 14). Joseph was witness to this, that is to say, he was not simply spectator of it, but he lived this mystery of Mary in his whole being. Hence we can understand that he could have been "madly" in love with Mary, yet not had a carnal love for her, as Saint Thomas suggests elsewhere: "Sanctifying grace not only suppressed in her all movements of sensuality; [this grace] was even efficacious for others, such that, as beautiful as she was in her body, Mary was never able to be desired [in a carnal way] by a man" (*Commentary on the Sentences*, III, Dist. 3, q. 1, a. 2, q. 1, ad 4).

292. Gen 29:9-11.

293. Jn 1:14.

294. This expression, frequently used by the prophets, occurs four times in Luke's Gospel: 1:68, 78; 7:16; 19:44.

295. Jn 1:14.

296. Lk 3:23 and 4:22; Jn 1:45 and 6:42.

297. Mt 13:55; Mk 6:3. Cf. Lk 3:23.

298. When was Joseph called to go and be with God? We do not know. We know only that he was still alive when Jesus was twelve years old. We may suppose that when Jesus was old enough to look after Mary Himself, Joseph stepped back in order to leave Mary and Jesus alone… Joseph surely lived something analogous to what John the Baptist lived: "He Who has the bride is the Bridegroom… He must increase, but I must decrease" (Jn 3:29-30). Joseph must surely have known this "perfect joy" of stepping back to let Jesus take precedence. We are not told this explicitly; it remains hidden in God—"For the works of the Lord are wonderful, and His works are concealed from men" (Sir 11:4). Whereas the Apostles are the "pillars" of the Church (cf. Gal 2:9 where Paul names Peter, James and John), Joseph is a *foundation* for the Church. Now the foundations of a building are always hidden. Perhaps this is the reason that Joseph was asked to disappear before the beginning of Jesus' apostolic life. Did Jesus ask this sacrifice of Joseph, so that he would be truly a foundation? We do not know; but what we can be sure of is that the following beatitude from the Book of Revelation may be applied to Joseph: "'Blessed are the dead who die in the Lord henceforth.' 'Blessed indeed,' says the Spirit, 'that they may rest from their labors, for their deeds follow them!'" (Rev 14:13). On Peter and Joseph, see note 163.

299. The only two phrases of Jesus concerning Mary—"Who is My mother?" in the synoptic Gospels (Mt 12:48-49; Mk 3:31-35; Lk 8:19-21) and "Blessed rather are those who hear the word of God and keep it" in Luke (11:28)—seem very impoverishing for Mary. But, in fact, these words must have been for her, in her poverty, the cause of a very great joy, since her only desire was indeed "to do the will of My Father Who is in heaven" (Mt 12:50) and to keep His word (cf. Lk 2:19, 51)—"If a man loves Me, he will keep My word, and My Father will love him, and We will come to him and make Our home with him" (Jn 14:23).

300. Mt 13:8, 23; Mk 4:8, 20; Lk 8:8, 15.

301. Song 8:5.

302. "She was indeed the Father's bride, the Mother of the Son and the dwelling place of the Holy Spirit" (*Fuit enim sponsa Patris, mater Filii, habitaculum Spiritus Sancti*). This statement in a sermon formerly attributed to Saint Thomas is perhaps not his own, since the sermon is no longer recognized as authentic, but it corresponds well to the way in which Saint Thomas sees Mary.

303. Saint Louis-Marie Grignon de Montfort wrote, "Mary is the excellent masterpiece of the Most High... the admirable Mother of the Son... the 'sealed fountain' (Song 4:12), the faithful spouse of the Holy Spirit, to whom He alone has entrance. Mary is the sanctuary and the repose of the Most Holy Trinity." *Treatise on the True Devotion* (Rockford, Ill.: TAN Books, 1985), no. 5, p. 4.

He clarifies this further, saying, "One of the great reasons why the Holy Spirit does not now do startling wonders in our souls is because He does not find there a sufficiently great union with His faithful and inseparable spouse. I say, 'inseparable' spouse, because since that Substantial Love of the Father and the Son has espoused Mary, in order to produce Jesus Christ, the Head of the elect, and Jesus Christ in the elect, He has never repudiated her, because she has always been fruitful and faithful" (ibid., no. 36, p. 21; see also nos. 20-21, 25, 34, 37, 49, 164, 217, 269). "As the Holy Ghost has espoused Mary and has produced in her, by her and from her, His masterpiece, Jesus Christ, the Word Incarnate, and has never repudiated His spouse, so He now continues to produce the elect, in her and by her, in a mysterious but real manner." *The Secret of Mary* (Rockford, Ill.: TAN Books, 1998), no. 13, p. 12; cf. nos. 15, 67, 68.

Saint Maximilian Mary Kolbe, for his part, says that the union between Mary and the Holy Spirit "is inexpressible, and so perfect that the Holy Spirit acts only by the Immaculata, His spouse. Hence she is the mediatrix of all the graces of the Holy Spirit." Letter of July 28, 1935, quoted by H.M. Manteau-Bonamy, O.P. in *Immaculate Conception and the Holy Spirit: The Marian Teachings of Saint Maximilian Kolbe*, trans. Bro. Richard Arnandez, F.S.C., (Libertyville, Ill.: Prow Books, 1977), pp. 40-41, 71. And again, "The Immaculata is so perfect, she is so closely united with the Holy Spirit that she can be called His *spouse*. This is why we consecrate everything to her. In her we find everything. She is, so to speak, the personification of the Holy Spirit." Conference of June 20, 1937, quoted by H.M. Manteau-Bonamy, op. cit., p. 105. Some days before his arrest, Fr. Kolbe even went so far as to say, "Our human word 'spouse' is far too weak to express the reality of the relationship between the Immaculata and the Holy Spirit. We can affirm that she is, in a certain sense, the 'incarnation' of the Holy Spirit. It is the Holy Spirit that we love in her, and through her, we love the Son." Conference of February 5, 1941, ibid., p. 50. Fr. Kolbe was well aware that we cannot speak of an "incarnation" of the Holy Spirit, even in Mary; yet we do not have the words capable of expressing such great mysteries. He says elsewhere—and this is very beautiful—that "our Holy Mother is, so to speak, one with the Holy Spirit." Conference of September 25, 1937, ibid., p. 102.

304. Cf. Eph 1:3-4: "Blessed be the God and Father of Our Lord Jesus Christ... He chose us in Him before the foundation of the world, that we should be holy and blameless before Him." The Vulgate translated the Greek term which means "blameless" as *immaculati*. Likewise in 5:27, Col. 1:22 and Rev 14:5 (*sine macula*) as well as in several psalms. The same Greek expression found in Phil 2:15, however, is translated as *sine reprehensione*.

305. Gen 2:18.

306. 1 Col 6:19.

307. See Ch. 4, pp. 97-98.

308. Mt 4:10 and Lk 4:8 (Deut 6:13); cf. Mt 22:37-38 and Mk 12:29-30.

309. See above, Part II, Ch. 1.

310. The Greek text of Mt 1:20 says "your woman" (*gunaika*). Cf. above, note 271.

APPENDIX

311. Reprinted here with permission from Saint Joseph's Oratory.

A NOTE ON THE TYPE

The text of this book is set in Arno. Named after the Florentine river which runs through the heart of the Italian Renaissance, Arno draws on the warmth and readability of early humanist typefaces of the 15th and 16th centuries.

MARIE-DOMINIQUE PHILIPPE (1912-2006) was a Dominican philosopher and theologian. He was ordained in 1936, and in 1945 was sent as a professor to the (Pontifical, Dominican) University of Fribourg (Switzerland), where he taught until 1982.

Alongside his teaching, Fr. Philippe gave lectures in philosophy and theology in very different environments—for family associations, business leaders, physicians, Christian trade unions, and artists. He wrote many books of philosophy and spiritual theology which cover a wide field of study and interest: reflections on mathematics and medicine, the philosophy of art, metaphysical studies, works on the family, as well as notable books on the Gospel of John, and the mystery of Christ and the Virgin Mary.

Although he remained a Dominican, he founded the Community of St. John in 1975. The Community is centered around adoration of Jesus in the Eucharist, devotion to Mary, and filial obedience to the successor of Peter in the person of the Holy Father.

Christ in His Mysteries by Bl. Columba Marmion. 466 pages, softcover: $21.95. The works of Marmion are "outstanding in the accuracy of their doctrine, the clarity of their style, and the depth and richness of their thought." — Pope Pius XII

"Spiritual reading at its best... One hopes that a new generation of readers will be helped by this work to discover the unfolding of the mystery of Christ." — Lawrence Cunningham, *Commonweal*

Loving and Living the Mass by Fr. Thomas Kocik. 88 pages, $7.95. "An excellent short treatment of the Mass for new Catholics and cradle Catholics as well. The author invites you to a real understanding of the Mass as a deeply spiritual event." — Fr. Benedict Groeschel

Priestblock 25487: A Memoir of Dachau by Fr. Jean Bernard. 197 pages, $14.95. "Stunning... Casts light into dark and previously neglected corners of the horror that was the Third Reich." — Richard John Neuhaus

"Fr. Jean Bernard's portrait of survival in a German concentration camp is simple, forceful and vivid and therefore impossible to put down or forget. *Priestblock 25487* is a diary of Catholic discipleship under extreme conditions that ranks with the great 20th Century personal testimonies against totalitarian violence." — Archbishop Chaput

"Many hundreds of books have been written about German concentration and extermination camps. Of these, *Priestblock 25487* is among the very best. Every scholar and student of that dreadful chapter of 20th-century history ought to read and ponder its contents." — John Lukacs, author *Five Days in London: May 1940*

"Riveting." — John Burger, *Nat'l Catholic Register*

"Absorbing... Beautifully written." — Erin Ryan, *Nat'l Cath. Rptr.*

"It is dramatic. It is brutally honest. I loved the book and could not put it down." — Teresa Tomeo, Ave Maria Radio

"Should be treated as a meditation, even something to be read again and again." — Barbara Stinson Lee, *Intermountain Catholic*

"A must-read for Catholics. Provides fresh anecdotal insight into the Vatican's battle against the Nazis." — Daniel Cole, *The Wanderer*